WORSHIP ON EARTH
AS IT IS IN HEAVEN

D1010425

Also by Rory Noland

The Heart of the Artist

Thriving as an Artist in the Church

The Worshiping Artist

WORSHIP ON EARTH AS IT IS IN HEAVEN

Exploring Worship
as a Spiritual Discipline

RORY NOLAND

ZONDERVAN.com/
AUTHORTRACKER
follow your favorite authors

ZONDERVAN

Worship on Earth as It Is in Heaven
Copyright © 2011 by Rory Noland

This title is also available as a Zondervan ebook. Visit www.zondervan.com/ebooks.

This title is also available in a Zondervan audio edition. Visit www.zondervan.fm.

Requests for information should be addressed to:
Zondervan, *Grand Rapids, Michigan* 49530

Library of Congress Cataloging-in-Publication Data

Noland, Rory.
  Worship on earth as it is in heaven : exploring worship as a spiritual
discipline / Rory Noland.
    p.   cm.
  Includes bibliographical references.
  ISBN 978-0-310-33128-5 (softcover)
  1. Worship. I. Title.
BV10.3.N65 2011
264 — dc22   2011006390

Cover design: Juicebox Designs
Interior design: Beth Shagene

Printed in the United States of America

11 12 13 14 15 16 /DCI/ 22 21 20 19 18 17 16 15 14 13 12 11 10 9 8 7 6 5 4 3 2 1

Contents

PART TWO

Growing as a Corporate Worshiper

Worship Now ... and Forever

"Rory, that song was too fast. I couldn't keep up."
"Rory, that song was way too slow. Felt like a dirge."
"Rory, you need to tell the drummer to quit banging so hard."
"Rory, those sound guys need to turn up the electric guitar."

Being involved in church music for most of my life, I've had my fair share of calls from congregation members complaining about the music.

Many years ago, I braced myself for yet another complaint when a call came through to me from a "long-time attender." It turned out to be a conversation I've never forgotten. The man on the other end of the phone asked me to recommend a voice teacher. I asked him how old the child was.

"No, no," he quickly said. "It's not for my kid, it's for me."

For some reason, I had assumed he was inquiring on behalf of one of his children. Suspecting that I had another aspiring American Idol on my hands, I probed deeper. "Are you wanting to join the choir or audition for the worship team?"

"No," he replied. "I just want to do a better job of worshiping on Sunday morning."

"Now let me get this straight," I said. "You want to pay for voice lessons just so you can sit out in the congregation on Sunday and sing better?"

"Something like that." He chuckled. "I've always used my inability to sing as an excuse not to worship. I don't really want to be a singer. I just want to become a better worshiper."

You may not need to run out and take voice lessons, but there's something to be learned from a man who is willing to invest time and money into improving his ability to worship.

Wanted: True Worshipers

God is looking for people who, like my friend on the phone, want to become better worshipers. John 4:23 tells us that God is looking for people who want to do more than just show up for worship. Jesus said, "But the hour is coming, and is now here, when the true worshipers will worship the Father in spirit and truth, for the Father is seeking such people to worship him." God is looking for "true worshipers"—people who mean business when it comes to worship. He seeks people who have a passion for God and aren't afraid to show it, who worship God for who he truly is and the way he wants to be worshiped, as revealed in the Bible. The goal of this book is to help you grow in your worship of God.

Obstacles to True Worship

Every Sunday, in churches all over the world, believers gather to worship. Yet, of all the spiritual disciplines, worship is the most misunderstood. To many, worship is synonymous with music — hymns or praise choruses. It's the part of a church service led by a "worship leader." To them, worship is something done within the church doors on Sunday morning.

Contributing to this narrow view of worship is the alarming lack of resources addressing the individual and corporate practice of worship. There are plenty of wonderful books that teach us how to pray, to fast, to read the Bible, and practice other spiritual disciplines, but not many instructing us on how to worship. There are also many books training worship leaders in how to plan and lead worship services. Even books about the theology of worship, while very important, don't always offer clear-cut suggestions on how to actually do it.

As a result, a lot of people sitting in church every Sunday don't know how or have difficulty truly engaging with God during worship. In a survey of Christians, George Barna reports that an alarming percentage of us are unable to encounter God in a meaningful way, especially at church:

> Eight out of every ten believers do not feel they have entered into the presence of God, or experience a connection with Him, during the worship service. Half of all believers say they do not feel they have entered into the presence of God or experienced a genuine connection with Him during the past year.[1]

Even those who sing and clap energetically during church may not be as focused as they look. My mind, for example, often wanders during worship to the point where I'm not even thinking about what I'm singing. Instead, I'll be thinking about where I'd like to go for lunch after church, some new song I heard on the radio, or why Chicago sports teams are perennial losers.

Truth is, many of us come to church weary and tired; we have a lot on our minds; we're easily distracted. In a fast-paced, entertainment-driven world like ours, many people don't know how to sit still, concentrate, and participate in worship. Furthermore, what goes on during a typical service—all the singing, standing, and clapping—may even seem foreign to some, especially to those who didn't grow up going to church.

To further complicate matters, many churches are struggling through "worship wars," with bitter battle lines drawn between traditional and contemporary, contemporary versus more contemporary, young versus old. One beleaguered pastor remarked to me recently that he doesn't know whether worship is worth all the trouble.

Overcoming the Obstacles

Though the challenges facing potential worshipers are numerous and far reaching, they are by no means insurmountable. *Worship on Earth as It Is in Heaven* addresses the challenges and offers a nuts-and-bolts approach, with practical suggestions gleaned from Scripture on how to worship.

The first half of this book explores what it means to grow as an *individual* worshiper. We'll analyze the worship practices of David, the psalmist, and learn how to worship God more effectively on our own, one-on-one. The second section discusses how to become a better *corporate* worshiper. Think of it as a guide on how to go to church. We'll examine the glorious worship gatherings in heaven as described in the book of Revelation and make suggestions you can take with you to church and apply every Sunday.

David was one who enjoyed worshiping on earth, but also looked forward to doing the same in heaven. In Psalm 145:1, he wrote, "I will extol you, my God and King, and bless your name forever and ever." As you read this book, my hope is that your individual and corporate worship will be enriched and that you will experience, as much as is humanly possible, worship on earth as it is in heaven.

A Word about the Word *Worship*

The word *worship* refers to an activity as well as a lifestyle. It speaks to something we do but also something we are — worshipers. Worship can be discussed in broad, general terms or as explicit action. This book will deal mostly with worship as an explicit action. Other than the third and fourth chapters, which discuss worship as a lifestyle, when I use the word *worship* I mean the actual act of expressing love, praise, and adoration to God.

How to Use This Book

This book is designed for both group study and personal reading. For group study, discussion questions are provided at the beginning of each chapter. In addition, application ideas appear under the heading "Ponder and Apply" at the end of every chapter. If you're reading this book alone, not as part of a small group, I suggest you journal about what you learn or share with a friend how the material in each chapter is helping you grow as a worshiper.

Worship on Earth as It Is in Heaven develops a few concepts first introduced in one of my previous books titled *The Worshiping Artist: Equipping You and Your Ministry Team to Lead Others in Worship*. For that reason, this book takes up where the previous one ended, summarizing pivotal concepts in the first chapter and then expounding on them throughout the remainder of the book. Should you desire further reading on the theology of worship or the role worship plays in spiritual formation, I humbly recommend *The Worshiping Artist* for consideration. Though that particular book was written for musicians and other artists, the basic concepts are relevant to all believers.

This book is written for the average Sunday worshiper, though there is a short section in every chapter especially for pastors and worship leaders because many of the issues we'll be discussing have implications for how churches plan services and lead worship. A thorough discussion is beyond the scope of this book, but I thought it might be helpful to at least pose questions to stimulate dialogue and offer suggestions on how leaders can begin to apply the material to their church settings.

Meeting an Urgent Need

Finally, I hope that pastors and worship leaders recommend this book to their congregations or suggest it for small group study. As a traveling consultant, I observe a large number of churches and worship services. I'm thrilled that worship and the arts are playing an increasing role in today's church, but one of the most disturbing trends I observe is that people sitting in our congregations are not participating as they should. While the worship team leads enthusiastically from the front, the majority of attenders, especially the men, stare off into space, not singing. No wonder the most common question I hear from church leaders is, "How can I get my people to engage more during worship?" Written especially with the average layperson in mind, this book addresses that question in a balanced, nonthreatening manner. Each chapter identifies a major "takeaway," or principle idea, that can be immediately applied to one's life. Given the high priority God places on worship, I can't think of a more urgent need in the church today than a clear understanding of worship as a spiritual discipline.

PART 1

Growing as a Private Worshiper

Worship in the Psalms of David

If a church wants to take the next step in improving its worship, it's not always necessary to overhaul the program or find a new worship leader. Instead, I would encourage every member to become individual worshipers. Can you imagine a church comprised largely of people who worshiped God on their own during the week and then came together on Sunday to worship? Their hearts would be so primed for worship, it wouldn't matter whether the music was traditional, contemporary, or whatever. Theologian D. A. Carson adds:

> In the same way that, according to Jesus, you cannot find yourself until you lose yourself, so also you cannot find excellent corporate worship until you stop trying to find excellent

corporate worship and pursue God himself. Despite the pro-
testations, one sometimes wonders if we are beginning to
worship *worship* rather than worship *God*. As a brother put it
to me, it's a bit like those who begin by admiring the sunset
and soon begin to admire themselves admiring the sunset.[2]

True worshipers experience more than great music or stirred
emotions during worship; they experience being in the presence
of God.

The Power and Privilege of Private Worship

The first step to becoming a better worshiper is to become a
vibrant worshiper Monday through Saturday. As believers, we
can worship God on our own, one-on-one, and experience the
power and privilege of worship every day.

A. W. Tozer emphatically underscores the importance of
daily individual worship:

> You will be worshiping God long after everything else has
> ceased to exist. Too bad if you do not learn to worship Him
> now so that you do not have to cram for the last examina-
> tion. For my part, I want to worship God in my own private
> life so fully and satisfyingly to the end so that I will not
> have to cram for the final exams. I can nearly stop breath-
> ing with quietness and say, "I worship Him; I am still wor-
> shiping Him; and I expect to worship Him for all eternity."
>
> That is what you are here for, to glorify God and enjoy
> Him thoroughly and forever, telling the universe how great
> God is.[3]

If you long to worship God "fully and satisfyingly to the
end" of your days, if you desire to worship God on a deeper

level, the Lord may be calling you to take the next step in your practice of personal worship.

David, the Private Worshiper

Other than Jesus, the best example of a day-to-day worshiper in the Bible is David. He was a king and a warrior, but he was also a poet and prolific songwriter. In fact, half of the 150 psalms are attributed to David, which means that he either wrote those particular psalms or is associated with them in some way. We don't know what David's music sounded like, but his lyrics have come down to us through the ages and are some of the most cherished and quoted portions of Scripture. David's psalms have been sung, prayed, recited, chanted, and dramatized through the centuries all over the world. Moreover, they cover the full range of human emotion, from anger and sadness to zeal and joy.

Even the psalms that didn't flow from David's pen still exhibit his influence. Asaph, for example, an ancient worship leader who wrote twelve psalms, was appointed by David, as were the sons of Korah, a Levitical family of worship leaders who authored eleven psalms. Two psalms are credited to King Solomon, David's son. No wonder Charles Spurgeon's voluminous commentary on the book of Psalms is aptly titled *The Treasury of David*, for this rich treasure chest of prayers, testimony, and song is closely identified with David and bound together by one central theme: worship.

Intensely Personal

For more than three thousand years, the psalms of David have been a mainstay in public worship gatherings, and yet many are intensely personal. David loved to spend time alone with

God. "For God alone my soul waits in silence," he declared (Psalm 62:1; see also Psalm 62:5). Throughout Psalm 37, David reminds us three times to wait on the Lord (Psalm 37:7, 9, 34). Though king over God's people, David understood that God is a personal God who values one-on-one time with his children.

David treasured intimacy with God. When David committed adultery and realized that he had sinned against God, his greatest fear was being alienated from God. "Cast me not away from your presence," he pleaded, "and take not your Holy Spirit from me" (Psalm 51:11). David couldn't imagine life apart from God and, more than anything, he wanted to be close to God.

That's why reading David's psalms often feels like an invasion of privacy, as if you're reading a personal diary or eavesdropping on someone's most private thoughts. Take Psalm 139:1–3 for example:

> O LORD, you have searched me and known me! You know when I sit down and when I rise up; you discern my thoughts from afar. You search out my path and my lying down and are acquainted with all my ways.

Like the example above, many of David's psalms are addressed or written directly to the Lord. "Hear my cry, O God, listen to my prayer; from the end of the earth I call to you when my heart is faint. Lead me to the rock that is higher than I, for you have been my refuge, a strong tower against the enemy" (Psalm 61:1–3). David's poetry not only speaks about God but it speaks to him as well.

Deeply Passionate

David was hungry for God. In Psalm 143:6, he wrote, "I stretch out my hands to you; my soul thirsts for you like a parched land." David's passion for God comes through loud and clear in his worship: "I give thanks to you, O Lord my God, with my whole heart, and I will glorify your name forever" (Psalm 86:12). Serious worshipers are known for their intense, passionate devotion to God.

A Life of Private Worship

I used to wonder where David learned to worship with such depth, intimacy, and passion. I now realize that it was during those early years he spent alone in the fields tending his father's sheep. In seclusion, alone with God, was where David truly learned how to worship. In several stages of life, we glimpse David worshiping God privately. Let's examine a few of these scenes, starting with those formative years as a young shepherd.

Shepherd Boy

In his younger days, it seems as though David and his sheep were inseparable. When Samuel came to anoint him king of Israel, David was out on the hillside herding the sheep (1 Samuel 16:11). Afterward, he didn't call a press conference or pose for photo ops; he went back to his shepherding duties. In fact, when Saul summoned David to play his harp in the royal court, he asked David's father, Jesse, to send his son "who is with the sheep" (1 Samuel 16:19). It's as if Saul said, "Hey, Jesse, send me that kid of yours who's really into sheep." When his brothers went off to war, David, being the youngest, was stuck at home guarding sheep (1 Samuel 17:15).

In 1 Samuel 17:34–36, David admitted to learning valuable combat lessons in the company of his wooly friends. Those fields were not only the training grounds where David became a warrior but they were also the schoolhouse where he learned to be a worshiper. After all, who else but a bona fide shepherd could have possibly written the Twenty-third Psalm? "The LORD is my shepherd.... He makes me lie down in green pastures. He leads me beside still waters" (Psalm 23:1–2). For every shepherd, a life of solitude comes with the job, and in David's case, it inspired deep heartfelt worship.

Middle-Aged King

As king, David wanted to honor God by building a temple for worship, but God rejected his offer. Extremely disappointed, Scripture reveals that David "went in and sat before the LORD" (2 Samuel 7:18). We will examine this story in more detail in chapter 4, but for now notice that when David heard the bad news, he immediately got alone with God. It was customary in those days to enlist the services of the high priest, a prophet, or some other religious professional. David went directly to God and worshiped.

Sage Old Man

David lived a long and fruitful life. He went from a worshiping shepherd boy to a worshiping king, so it was only natural for him to be worshiping at the end of his days. For example, in Psalm 143:5, David looks back on his life and is encouraged by all that God has done: "I remember the days of old; I meditate on all that you have done; I ponder the work of your hands."

Upon his deathbed, there was chaos and confusion as to who would be David's successor. Finally his son, Solomon, was anointed king. When David's servants came to congratulate him, his response was one of praise to God: "Blessed be the LORD, the God of Israel, who has granted someone to sit on my throne this day, my own eyes seeing it" (1 Kings 1:48).

Enrolling in David's School of Private Worship

Over the next four chapters, David will serve as mentor and guide in our quest to grow as private worshipers. We will examine four compelling characteristics of David's private worship and glean practical principles we can apply to our own individual efforts. We will see that David practiced the following in his worship:

- Made worship his top priority
- Observed a regular routine of private worship
- Regarded obedience as the highest form of worship
- Worshiped amidst adversity

David may be a prime example of a biblical worshiper, but he is not a perfect example. He struggled with sexual lust, committed adultery and murder, and tried to cover it up. On top of all that, David wasn't an exemplary father. He failed to discipline his children (2 Samuel 13:21), and he wasn't attentive to them either (2 Samuel 14:24, 28). So, much like you and me, David was greatly flawed, prone to weaknesses, and saddled with shortcomings. Yet he continually sought the Lord in worship.

Of course, our study will not be confined to merely the Old Testament. We'll learn all we can from Jesus, the disciples, the apostle Paul, and others, for they too have something significant to add to our discussion of private worship.

Lay Aside False Assumptions

Before we get started, however, it's important to discard any and all assumptions you have regarding worship. David learned that lesson the hard way. During his reign as king, David made arrangements to move the ark of the covenant to its final resting place in Jerusalem. The ark played a significant role in Old Testament worship; it's where God manifested his presence. David assumed he could just put the ark on a cart and roll it down the street. During the trip, though, the cart hit a bump in the road, and a man named Uzzah, who was part of the procession, reached out his hand to steady the ark. God immediately struck down Uzzah, and he died on the spot. David was so upset, he temporarily called off the entire operation (2 Samuel 6:2–10).

At first glance, Uzzah's punishment seems unfair for what seemed like a good deed. But the rescue mission blatantly violated God's commands. Earlier in Scripture, God clearly stipulated that whenever the ark was to be moved, it had to be carried by the Levites—hoisted on their shoulders using poles placed through several rings on the sides of the ark (see Exodus 25:14–15; Numbers 7:9). Furthermore, Numbers 4:15 adamantly forbids anyone to ever touch the ark. Had David followed God's prescribed rules, a lot of pain and tragedy could have been avoided.

Like Uzzah, many of us have assumptions and practices that may be well-intentioned but false, based on tradition, upbringing, or personal preference. When we operate on false assumptions, we fail to properly honor God.

Search the Scriptures

Eventually, David searched the Scriptures, or someone brought them to his attention, and he learned the correct way to transport the ark (see 2 Samuel 6:12–15). We too need to scour the Bible to learn how God wants to be worshiped. For it doesn't matter how you and I want to praise God. It's not ultimately important whether worship makes us feel good or if the music is to our liking. True worship must always be offered on God's terms, not ours. So we need to learn how God wants to be worshiped. In this book, we will continually come back to the Bible as the only source of truth and information regarding worship.

David certainly possessed a high view of God's Word. In Psalm 138:2, he reverently stated, "For you have exalted above all things your name and your word." "The word of the LORD proves true," he wrote (Psalm 18:30).

> The law of the LORD is perfect, reviving the soul; the testimony of the LORD is sure, making wise the simple; the precepts of the LORD are right, rejoicing the heart; the commandment of the LORD is pure, enlightening the eyes.
>
> PSALM 19:7–8

Because of his deep respect for God's Word, David was open to its teaching and his own worship was biblically based. In Psalm 32, God warns us, through David, not to be obstinate, but to gladly receive godly instruction:

> I will instruct you and teach you in the way you should go; I will counsel you with my eye upon you. Be not like a horse or a mule, without understanding, which must be curbed with bit and bridle, or it will not stay near you.
>
> PSALM 32:8–9

Christians can be stubborn as mules, set in their ways, especially when it comes to worship. Let's you and I respond differently by laying aside long-held notions and searching the Scriptures to learn all we can about how God desires to be worshiped. As we begin our journey, may we hear and heed David's invitation to "taste and see that the Lord is good" (Psalm 34:8), with eager anticipation for all that God's Word has to teach us about growing as worshipers of Father, Son, and Holy Spirit.

CHAPTER 1

Do What Matters Most
Make Worship a Priority

On Sunday morning, the Johnson family drives to church at the other end of town. Ned, proud father of the three boys in the back seat, works an office job during the week. Nellie, his wife, works part time as a substitute teacher. Together, Ned and Nellie lead a small group at the church and volunteer with the high school group.

As they drive along the interstate, the conversation is usually punctuated with loving directives toward the back seat to stop yelling, whining, and hitting. This morning, however, the boys are unusually quiet, behaving like model citizens.

"Did you slip them tranquilizers?" Ned whispers to Nellie.

"No, they're just tired from the party yesterday," she answers.

"That makes four of us," Ned says.

"No, five," Nellie adds. "I'm pretty worn out myself. The Browns sure know how to throw a party, though, don't they?"

"Yeah, all day and all night." Ned moans. "If that was their kid's tenth birthday, what are they gonna do when he turns sixteen, or eighteen, or graduates? I mean, how do you top lunch at the bowling alley, a ballgame, a movie, and then Chuck E. Cheese for dinner? What do you do next year?"

"Billy's an only child, you know," Nellie says.

"Yeah, I know. But that's still too much, don't you think?" Nellie nods in agreement.

"Must have cost a fortune," Ned says. As he slows down for the exit ramp, he glances at his rearview mirror into the back seat. "I think Jason's asleep," he whispers.

Sure enough, little Jason is slumped over in his car seat.

"Mom, Jason's drooling," gripes Nathan, their oldest.

Nellie, prepared as usual, whips out an assortment of wipes and tissues, mops and dabs Jason's face, and then props him back up in his seat, all without waking him.

"Do you know who's preaching today?" Ned asks.

"I think it's Pastor Jim," Nellie says.

"Oh, no." Ned groans. "I love Pastor Jim, but he's so dry, and he always goes long. If I don't stop for coffee, I'll be snoring and drooling through the sermon myself."

"We don't have time to stop, dear."

"I'll go through the drive-up. It'll only take a second," Ned assures her.

Unfortunately, the line for the drive-up window is five cars deep. To make matters worse, the woman directly ahead of the Johnsons sends her order back, adding further delay. By the time Ned has coffee in hand, church is starting, just a few blocks away. Ned can tell his wife is perturbed.

"Sorry," Ned offers. "I'll step on it and get us there in no time."

"Don't bother, we're already late."

"You have that 'I told you so' look again."

"Well, I told you not to stop for coffee."

"How was I supposed to know that everybody and their brother would stop for coffee at the same time, at the same place? Obviously, the whole church is getting caffeinated to make it through the sermon."

"Very funny."

"Really, I don't know what the big deal is," Ned says. "We're only a few minutes late."

"I hate to be late," Nellie protests. "By the time we park, unload, and get the kids in their classes, we'll be ten minutes late."

"I promise it'll be five minutes at the most." Ned is trying to sound conciliatory.

"I don't want to miss five minutes of the service," Nellie insists.

"Well, I guarantee you we won't miss the sermon," Ned persists. "Even if it's boring, it's the most important—the real meat of the service. I don't think it'll kill us to miss a few minutes at the beginning. It's just worship."

Discussion Questions

1 What does Ned's apparent lack of concern for arriving late to church communicate about the priority he places on worship?

2 What do you think causes someone like Ned to place such low value on worship?

3 How common do you think is Ned's opinion of worship among church attendees today?

4 What other attitudes, statements, or actions on the part of Christians indicate a low regard for worship?

5 How common is Ned's belief that the sermon is the most important part of the service? Do you agree or disagree with that?

Top Priority

"One thing have I asked of the LORD, that will I seek after: that I may dwell in the house of the LORD all the days of my life, to gaze upon the beauty of the LORD and to inquire in his temple" (Psalm 27:4). David's devotion to worship oozes from this verse. More than anything, David wanted to bask in the beauty of God's presence. He was enamored with God's glory. The "one thing" David longs for is intimacy with God and a chance to worship his heavenly Father. As you probably picked up from the car ride with the Johnsons, that first principle we discover about David's worship involves priorities. David made worship his top priority.

Because worship was such a high priority for David, he bristled whenever God wasn't given the honor he deserved. What stirred David to take on Goliath was not the threat he posed to Israel but the giant's blatant disrespect for Jehovah, Israel's God. David asked angrily, "Who is this uncircumcised Philistine, that he should defy the armies of the living God?" (1 Samuel 17:26). God's glory and reputation were at stake, and David felt compelled to take action. Upon confronting the Terminator from Gath, David shouted, "This day the LORD will deliver you into my hand … that all the earth may know that there is a God in Israel" (1 Samuel 17:46). You can always discern your priorities, for better or worse, by what angers you or stirs you, what frustrates you and what excites you. Honoring God was the utmost priority for David.

As king, David's reign over Israel was marked significantly by the prominent attention he gave to worship. He brought the ark of the covenant to Jerusalem and endeavored to build a temple because he wanted to restore worship as the centerpiece of Jewish life. David was also the first to incorporate music as a regular fixture in Israel's worship. He appointed singers and instrumentalists (1 Chronicles 15:16–24; 16:4–7; 25:1–8; 2 Chronicles 8:14), formed bands and choirs (2 Chronicles 29:25–26), pioneered antiphonal singing where one group sings and another echoes in response (Nehemiah 12:24), and even introduced new instruments into the worship service (1 Chronicles 23:5). On occasion, David even led his people in worship (1 Chronicles 16:8–36; 29:10–22). Israel never had a king as devoted to worshiping God as David was.

Why Make Worship a Priority?

David made worship a priority because he understood that we are created, commanded, called, compelled, and destined to worship. Because God was his ultimate priority, worship was his primary activity.

Created to Worship

In Isaiah, God refers to his people as those who are "called by my name, whom I created for my glory" and those "I formed for myself that they might declare my praise" (Isaiah 43:7, 21). First Peter 2:9 confirms that you and I were created to worship God: "But you are a chosen [people], a royal priesthood, a holy nation, a people for his own possession, *that you may proclaim the excellencies* of him who called you out of darkness into his marvelous light" (emphasis added). If you love to worship, if it feels right to you, it's because you're doing what you were created to do.

Commanded to Worship

I recently overheard someone contend that worship is not his "pathway to God." Not much of a singer, he admits to having trouble sensing God's presence and connecting with God during worship. Because this man equates worship solely with music, he could take it or leave it. "It's not really my thing," he said.

No matter our level of musical abilities, the Bible commands us to worship the Lord. David writes, "You who fear the LORD, praise him! All you offspring of Jacob, glorify him, and stand in awe of him, all you offspring of Israel!" (Psalm 22:23). Psalm 135:1 implores us, "Praise the LORD! Praise the name of the LORD, give praise, O servants of the LORD." The book of Psalms ends with this resounding imperative: "Let everything that has breath praise the LORD!" (Psalm 150:6).

Worship, therefore, is not optional; it is clearly commanded.

Called to Worship

As believers, worship is not merely something we do. It is who we are. In Jonah 1:9, the prophet proclaims, "I am a Hebrew and I worship the LORD, the God of heaven" (NIV). The apostle Paul said, "I worship the God of our fathers" (Acts 24:14). Both men regarded worship as a vital part of their identities. Being men of faith meant that they were called to worship God. Similarly, in Acts 16:14, there's a woman named Lydia who's described as "a worshiper of God." The same is said of a man named Titius Justus in Acts 18:7. Both of these first-century believers saw themselves as worshipers and were regarded by others as such.

Philippians 3:3 points out that true believers are ones who "worship by the Spirit of God and glory in Christ Jesus." A. W. Tozer confirms that "we are saved to worship God. All that Christ has done for us in the past and all that He is doing now leads to this one end."[4] If you are a believer, you are a worshiper; it is part of your new lifestyle as a follower of Christ.

Compelled to Worship

Some time ago, I heard a worship leader tell a group of young people that they needed to worship loud enough to make God smile. Though he meant well, the leader unfortunately made God sound childish and egotistical, as if he sits up in heaven pouting unless we flatter him with praise. Does God need us to worship him? Is he so insecure that he needs us to tell him how great and wonderful he is all the time? The answer is no to both questions. Acts 17:24–25 tells us:

> The God who made the world and everything in it, being Lord of heaven and earth, does not live in temples made by man, nor is he served by human hands, as though he needed anything, since he himself gives to all mankind life and breath and everything.

God doesn't need anything; he's God. He delights in our worship, but the truth is, we're the ones who need to worship.

C. S. Lewis contends that we delight to worship and we can't help doing it.[5] In Psalm 35:28, David exclaimed, "Then my tongue shall tell of your righteousness and of your praise all the day long." The author of Psalm 146 expresses a similar compulsion to worship: "I will praise the LORD as long as I live; I will sing praises to my God while I have my being" (Psalm 146:2). When we truly encounter God, we are enamored with his glory and can't help but overflow with joy. As C. S. Lewis says:

> The Scotch catechism says that man's chief end is "to glorify God and enjoy Him forever." But . . . these are the same thing. Fully to enjoy is to glorify. In commanding us to glorify Him, God is inviting us to enjoy Him.[6]

At its most basic level, worship is an exciting opportunity and a holy invitation to enjoy God.

Destined to Worship

Worship is one of the primary activities of heaven (see Revelation 4 – 5; 14:6 – 7; 19:10; 22:8 – 9). As the psalms announce, "We will give thanks to your name forever" (Psalm 44:8), because "his praise endures forever!" (Psalm 111:10). Biblical scholar N. T. Wright asserts:

> The great multitude in Revelation which no man can number aren't playing cricket. They are *worshipping.* Sounds boring? If so, it shows how impoverished our idea of worship has become.... Worship is the central characteristic of the heavenly life; and that worship is focused on the God we know in and as Jesus.[7]

We will study worship in heaven at greater length in the second part of this book, but for now suffice it to say that worship is one of the few things we're currently doing that we will do forever —all the more reason to make it a priority in our lives.

Worship Encompasses All of Life

Jesus introduced a whole new approach to worship. Believers were no longer required to make ceremonial blood sacrifices in the temple as stipulated in the Old Testament. Jesus became our sacrifice. "But when Christ had offered for all time a single sacrifice for sins, he sat down at the right hand of God" (Hebrews 10:12). Because Christ offered himself to God as the sacrifice of death for us on the cross, we are invited to offer ourselves to God as a "living sacrifice." The apostle Paul wrote, "I appeal to you therefore, brothers, by the mercies of God, to present your bodies as a living sacrifice, holy and acceptable to God, which is your spiritual worship" (Romans 12:1). Every breathing moment, we are invited to live in the presence of God and enjoy fellowship with him.

Colossians 3:17 implores us to do all we do for God's glory: "And whatever you do, in word or deed, do everything in the name of the Lord Jesus." Worship, therefore, encompasses all of life. It is as much Monday through Saturday as it is Sunday. "I will bless the LORD at all times; his praise shall continually be in my mouth," David wrote in Psalm 34:1. First Corinthians 10:31 says, "So, whether you eat or drink, or whatever you do, do all to the glory of God." Mark Driscoll writes:

> Worship is not merely an aspect of our being but the essence of our being as God's image bearers. As a result, all of life is ceaseless worship. Practically, this means that while worship does include corporate church meetings, singing songs, and liturgical forms, it is not limited by these things, defined solely as these things, or expressed only in these things, because worship never stops.[8]

Therefore, *everything* we do (working, playing, raising a family, repairing the car, going to school, serving at church, etc.) can be done as an act of worship.

Take your job, for example. What would it look like for you to turn your workplace into a place of worship? In a workshop setting, I once challenged the class to identify the part of their jobs that they hate the most and do that as an act of worship. A young man who worked at Starbucks confessed that he vehemently hated cleaning the toilets at work. That week, however, he became determined to do his job for the Lord, as worship. "I was not only more excited about going to work," he shared, "I took my job seriously and did it the best I could." Then he proudly added, "And when I was done cleaning those toilets, they never looked that good before." Understanding even the mundane aspects of our jobs as acts of worship brings new energy to our work (and cleaner toilets for customers!).

Worship Is God's Ultimate Priority

We must make worship a top priority because worship is God's ultimate priority. God is passionate about his glory. He says, "I am the LORD; that is my name; my glory I give to no other, nor my praise to carved idols" (Isaiah 42:8). The very first commandment stipulates that God be glorified above all other gods (Exodus 20:3). God is not willing to share his glory with another because it properly belongs to him as the one true living God.

The Bible's Top Priority

Smack dab in the middle of God's Word is a hymnal, a collection of praise songs known as the book of Psalms—the longest book of the Bible. Its length and location reflect the fact that, from Genesis to Revelation, Scripture's top priority is worship. In fact, the closer we look, the more we discover how prominent worship is throughout the biblical narrative.

Those who witnessed the birth of Christ were worshipers in the best sense of the word. When informed that she would give birth to the Messiah, Mary sang, "My soul magnifies the Lord, and my spirit rejoices in God my Savior" (Luke 1:46–47). At the birth of his son, who eventually became John the Baptist, Zechariah's first words were those of praise: "Blessed be the Lord God of Israel, for he has visited and redeemed his people" (Luke 1:68). The angels who appeared to the shepherds proclaimed, "Glory to God in the highest" (Luke 2:14). The wise men saw the baby Jesus and "fell down and worshiped him" (Matthew 2:11). Though it's often lost amidst all the hype and materialism today, worship permeates the Christmas story as it does all of Scripture.

God's Purpose Is Always His Glory

God's ultimate purpose for everything he does is always his glory.

God showed mercy to an unfaithful nation of Israel with the following explanation: "For my own sake, for my own sake, I do it" (Isaiah 48:11). God answers prayer and meets needs in order to manifest his glory. "And my God will supply every need of yours according to his riches in glory in Christ Jesus" (Philippians 4:19).

Furthermore, the purpose behind the plan of redemption is God's glory:

> In love he predestined us for adoption as sons through Jesus Christ ... *to the praise of his glorious grace.*
>
> EPHESIANS 1:4–6, EMPHASIS ADDED

> In him we have obtained an inheritance ... so that we who were the first to hope in Christ might be *to the praise of his glory.*
>
> EPHESIANS 1:11–12, EMPHASIS ADDED

> [We are] sealed with the promised Holy Spirit ... *to the praise of his glory.*
>
> EPHESIANS 1:13–14, EMPHASIS ADDED

As unusual as it may sound, God's ultimate purpose is not that we be saved but that he be glorified.[9] Redemption is not all about us; it's all about God. We are saved so that we can know and proclaim God's glory. That's why Paul referred to the gospel as the "glory of the blessed God" (1 Timothy 1:11).

God's deepest motivation is always his glory. "For from him and through him and to him are all things. To him be glory forever. Amen" (Romans 11:36). At this point, we need to be careful not to project human characteristics and tendencies onto God. A human being motivated by self-glorification would be a self-centered, overbearing egomaniac—driven by greed, insecurity, selfishness, and lust. Thankfully, God is nothing like us. He is holy, righteous, good, gracious, loving, and merciful. By virtue of his very being, God is worthy of our highest praise. He deserves our deepest reverence and awe.

Jesus' Top Priority

Theologian Noel Due contends that

> the issue of worship was not (and is not) a peripheral issue in the life of the Son of God, but lies at its very core. It is the key on which all hinges, not just for his own sake, but for the sake of the whole of the creation. All of Jesus' life was an expression of his worship to God his Father as he served him in thought, word and deed, and ultimately as he set the captives free from Satan's power through his sacrificial death.[10]

Scripture affirms that Jesus made worship his top priority. When asked which is the greatest of all the commandments, Jesus pointed to the one most directly associated with worship. He answered, "You shall love the Lord your God with all your heart and with all your soul and with all your mind. This is the great and first commandment" (Matthew 22:37 – 38). The Bible teaches that Jesus was crucified to bring God glory. Referring to his own death, Jesus said, "Now is the Son of Man glorified, and God is glorified in him" (John 13:31). He was raised from the dead "by the glory of the Father" (Romans 6:4), and when he returns, "the glory of our great God and Savior Jesus Christ" will appear (Titus 2:13). Jesus glorified the Father in everything he did.

What Happens When Worship Becomes a Priority?

If we are created, commanded, called, compelled, and destined to worship, and worship encompasses all of life and is God's ultimate priority, then worshiping God merits the utmost attention in our lives and produces a change in our behavior. Intentional priorities always transform the way we live. I have workaholic tendencies, so early in my marriage I resolved to spend quality time with my wife and two sons. When I make marriage and family a priority, it has practical effects. I leave the office at quitting time, I try not to bring work home, I plan "date nights," and I take the boys on outings. As we watch David make worship a priority, we get to see the inevitable effect it had. He experienced an increased awareness of God's presence, increased delight in God's attributes, and increased desire to be changed into the image of Christ.

Increased Awareness of God's Presence

David was convinced that there was absolutely no place he could go and no circumstance he could encounter that could put him out of God's reach. "Where shall I go from your Spirit?" he asked the Lord. "Or where shall I flee from your presence?" (Psalm 139:7).

> If I ascend to heaven, you are there! If I make my bed in Sheol, you are there! If I take the wings of the morning and dwell in the uttermost parts of the sea, even there your hand shall lead me, and your right hand shall hold me. If I say, "Surely the darkness shall cover me, and the light about me be night," even the darkness is not dark to you; the night is bright as the day, for darkness is as light with you.
>
> PSALM 139:8–12

God, therefore, is omnipresent—he is everywhere all the time. According to Acts 17:27, "He is actually not far from each one of us." So we don't have to beg God to come down from heaven and be with us or strain to climb up to him. He is Immanuel, God with us. According to C. S. Lewis,

> We may ignore, but we can nowhere evade, the presence of God. The world is crowded with Him. He walks everywhere

incognito. And the *incognito* is not always hard to penetrate. The real labour is to remember, to attend. In fact, to come awake. Still more, to remain awake.[11]

So it's never a question of how present God seems to us, *but how present we are to God.*

Worship increases our awareness of God's presence. David believed that God inhabits the praises of his people. Our worship does not lead us into God's presence; Jesus does! "For Christ also suffered once for sins, the righteous for the unrighteous, that he

---

TAKEAWAY #1: **Make Worship a Priority**

Are you experiencing an ever-increasing awareness of God's presence in your life? Are you noticing increased delight in the attributes of God? Is worship changing you into the image of Christ?

There was a time in my life when I would have answered no to each of those questions. I was having regular devotions — reading my Bible and praying every day. I was trying to obey God's Word and follow the Holy Spirit. However, I certainly couldn't say that worship was a priority in my life. As a result, I often struggled to know and feel God's presence, especially amidst the fast pace of the workplace. And I was working for a church at the time!

Truth is, at night, as I lay my head on the pillow, exhausted from a full day of meetings and appointments, I felt lonely for God. Just sixteen hours earlier, I had enjoyed meaningful fellowship with God. I had spent quality time in his Word and in prayer. I reveled in a strong sense of God's presence, but then quickly moved on to the next thing in my busy routine. By

---

might bring us to God" (1 Peter 3:18). So while worship, in and of itself, doesn't summon God's presence, it reminds us that God is continually near.

David was keenly aware of God's presence amidst his daily activities. He wrote, "I have set the LORD always before me; because he is at my right hand, I shall not be shaken" (Psalm 16:8). Confidence in God's presence strengthened David for the challenges he faced throughout his life. No wonder David valued and enjoyed God's presence so much. In Psalm 65:4, he exclaimed, "Blessed is the one you choose and bring near."

mid-morning, I couldn't remember much about my morning devotions, let alone draw any lasting sense of God's presence from them. Intentionally injecting more worship into my devotions and into my life freed me to experience God's presence in deeper, more meaningful life-changing ways.

Like Bible reading and prayer and the time you spend on them, you can tell how much of a priority worship is in your life by how much you do it and how deeply it penetrates your soul. If you're just starting out as a worshiper, perhaps only worshiping Sunday morning at church, the ensuing chapters offer practical ways you can incorporate worship into your daily routine.

Whether you're a beginner or a seasoned veteran of the faith, I challenge you, on the authority of God's Word, to make worship your top priority. Growing as a worshiper begins with a commitment to worship. I trust you are ready and willing to make that commitment today and reap the benefits for a lifetime and into eternity.

Increased Delight in God's Attributes

When artists paint a subject, they first study it carefully, noticing every detail, in order to capture it accurately on canvas. The true artist looks intently at the subject, coming back to it often, learning and discovering as much as possible so as to produce an authentic representation. In the same way, it's essential that you and I establish and cultivate a biblically correct concept of God.

Our image of God affects everything—how we think, act, even how we feel. And Satan will always tell us lies about God —that God isn't good or doesn't have our best interests at heart. Jesus taught that we are to worship the Lord "in spirit and truth" (John 4:23). Worshiping in truth means that we worship God for who he truly is, as revealed in Scripture. Just as a fine artist keeps returning to the model, we regularly contemplate the attributes of God to assure an accurate and awe-inspiring picture of God.

I've heard people say the strangest things while trying to describe their impressions of God's presence during worship. One time after a service, a young woman gushed that the worship time made her feel "warm and tingly all over" (which totally creeped me out). An obviously artistic woman once told me that the worship time "felt like corduroy" to her. I still have no idea what she meant. Then there was the man who came up to me after church, thanked me profusely for leading worship, and said, "God's presence was very real today." When I probed further, he shrugged his shoulders and said, "I don't know. I just felt it in the air." I couldn't tell what exactly "it" was that this man experienced.

God's presence may be difficult to describe and shrouded in mystery, but it's more than something in the air, more than a "feel good" experience, and more than the "warm fuzzy" before a hard-hitting sermon. To sense God's presence more often and more profoundly, we must delve deeper into God's character.

Experience God, Experience His Character

Simply put, worship is our response to the presence of God made possible by Jesus. However, it is not some general notion of God that captivates us, but most often a specific quality, or attribute. "For his invisible attributes, namely, his eternal power and divine nature, have been clearly perceived, ever since the creation of the world" (Romans 1:20). God's attributes are clear. As we grow as worshipers, we notice those attributes and praise God for them.

For David, encountering God's presence meant experiencing God's character—not hazy notions or sappy feelings about God's presence. Instead, God's presence was defined by his attributes, which explains why God's characteristics seem to roll easily off David's tongue. Take this praise offering from Psalm 36:5–7 for example:

> Your steadfast love, O LORD, extends to the heavens, your faithfulness to the clouds. Your righteousness is like the mountains of God; your judgments are like the great deep; man and beast you save, O LORD. How precious is your steadfast love, O God!

The names and attributes of God, therefore, are foundational to worship. We worship God for who he is, and the more we become acquainted with his many wonders, the richer our experience will be. When David dedicated the temple, he burst into a litany of God's attributes:

> Yours, O LORD, is the greatness and the power and the glory and the victory and the majesty, for all that is in the heavens and in the earth is yours. Yours is the kingdom, O LORD, and you are exalted as head above all. Both riches and honor come from you, and you rule over all. In your hand are power

and might, and in your hand it is to make great and to give
strength to all.

1 CHRONICLES 29:11–12

After calling out, in rapid-fire succession, one attribute of God
after another, David paused to catch his breath and then capped
it off with an exclamation point: "And now we thank you, our
God, and praise your glorious name" (1 Chronicles 29:13). David
delighted in God's attributes.

Cultivate an Accurate Picture of God

Being well schooled in the attributes of God deepened David's
love for God. Psalm 18 is a celebration of God's deliverance from
harm and difficulty. Yet, it begins affectionately. David simply
says, "I love you, O LORD, my strength" (Psalm 18:1). It's as if
David is saying, "Let me tell you what I love about the Lord. I
love his strength." Then, true to form, David enthusiastically
cites more attributes of God: "The LORD is my rock and my fortress and my deliverer, my God, my rock, in whom I take refuge,
my shield, and the horn of my salvation, my stronghold" (Psalm
18:2). Increased awareness of God's presence produces increased
delight in God's attributes.

Increased Desire to Be Changed

Every encounter with God comes with an invitation to act in
accordance with his character and will, to "put on the new self,
which is being renewed in knowledge after the image of its creator" (Colossians 3:10). Similarly, 2 Corinthians 3:18 teaches that
when we behold or contemplate God's glory, we "are being trans-
formed into the same image."

Throughout Psalm 139, David extols God for being omni-
scient, omnipresent, the Eternal Creator, and altogether wise.
Then he invites God to scrutinize his life and show him anything

that needs to change: "Search me, O God and know my heart! Try me and know my thoughts! And see if there be any grievous way in me, and lead me in the way everlasting!" (Psalm 139:23–24). On another occasion, David prayed, "Prove me, O LORD, and try me; test my heart and my mind. For your steadfast love is before my eyes, and I walk in your faithfulness" (Psalm 26:2–3). While contemplating the attributes of God, David was brought to a point of submission and surrender. "Teach me to do your will," David prayed, "for you are my God!" (Psalm 143:10).

God reveals himself to us, displaying his attributes and inviting us to reflect his image, to be like Christ. So as we worship, pondering God's divine qualities, may we, like David, be brought to a point of submission and allow those attributes to shape us and change us.

Ponder and Apply

1 At this point, what do you think it would mean for you to make worship a greater priority in your life?

2 What would it look like for you to do your job (or your schooling) as an act of worship?

3 Why are the attributes of God foundational to worship?

4 Why is it important to have a biblically accurate concept of God?

5 Read Psalm 111 and/or 145, in which are listed several attributes of God. Choose the one attribute you feel you need the most in your life right now and spend a few minutes in worship and prayer with that attribute as your theme.

FOR PASTORS AND WORSHIP LEADERS

I currently serve as pastor of worship at Harvest Bible Chapel, one church with six campuses throughout the Chicago area, under the leadership of Dr. James MacDonald. In one of my initial meetings with Pastor James, he introduced his views on worship by emphatically saying, "Worship is as important, if not more important, than my messages." Here was a world-class preacher and Bible teacher firmly asserting worship as a high value in our philosophy of ministry. As a result, worship is one of the pillars of our church.

Contrast Pastor James's strong convictions regarding worship with the minister who once told me that if it were up to him, there'd be no music in the service at all; that he'd preach the entire time. This pastor thought nothing of walking in halfway through the worship set, didn't visibly engage, and was often seen talking or joking around during tender moments of worship. Obviously, worship wasn't given prominence at that man's church.

Since worship is God's ultimate priority, then worship needs to be the top priority of every church. A. W. Tozer wrote,

> The Christian church exists to worship God first of all. Every-thing else must come second or third or fourth or fifth.... I believe a local church exists to do corporately what each Christian believer should be doing individually—and that is to worship God.[12]

Given the significance of worship, we leaders must diligently put together services that are purposeful and impacting. That's exactly the type of service Paul describes in 1 Corinthians 14:24–25:

> But if all prophesy, and an unbeliever or outsider enters, he is convicted by all, he is called to account by all, the secrets of his heart are disclosed, and so, falling on his face, he will worship God and declare that God is really among you.

It's important to remember that Paul is describing a church service, one in which the Holy Spirit is at work transforming lives. Believers and unbelievers alike are impacted to the core of their being. They're convicted of sin and called to repentance. Awe-struck by the greatness of God, they fall on their faces and worship him. Notice that the two main ingredients for a high-impact service are worship and the preaching of God's Word (prophecy). Worship truly is as important as the sermon.

CHAPTER 2

Make It a Habit
Establish a Regular Routine

It's that time of the month again for Natalie — that time that puts her on edge, causes anxiety, and turns her into a grumpy witch. I'm referring, of course, to that time of the month when she pays bills — that biweekly exercise in stretching her paycheck as far as it can go.

Natalie works full time at a local factory and as a waitress three nights a week and every other weekend. "Easy come, easy go," she says sarcastically as she organizes invoices and receipts on the kitchen table. She begins by bringing her checkbook up to date and then pays the rent. After that, Natalie puts the bills in order of due date and anxiously hopes there's enough to cover it all.

"Mom, I'm ready." That angelic voice belongs to Natalie's little girl, the love of her life, her pride and joy. In fact, that's her name — Joy. Very fitting for a cute little ten-year-old with Coke-bottle glasses, a pixie haircut, and a perpetual smile.

"I'll be there in a second, sweetie," Natalie calls. She signs another check, seals it in an envelope, and rushes to the bathroom. "Did you wash behind your ears and brush the back of your teeth?" she asks.

Joy nods.

"Good girl," Natalie says. "Time for bed." Natalie tucks Joy in, then lies beside her and reads to her for a while. They always end their day praying together, holding hands.

As Natalie turns out the light and heads for the door, Joy says, "Mommy, I don't wanna get braces."

"I know, honey, but you need them."

"But they're ugly," Joy blurts out.

"Well, it'll be a while before you get braces," Natalie says, "and you won't have to wear them long. You know, Mommy had braces for four years and look how straight my teeth are now." She flips the light back on and opens her mouth wide. Then she sticks out her tongue and they both laugh. "Besides," Natalie continues, "nothing could ever make you ugly. Don't ever forget that."

Joy smiles.

Natalie gives her a hug and another good-night kiss before lights out.

She returns to the pile of bills on the kitchen table. She knocks out a couple more while keeping a wary eye on the balance. Her cell phone rings. It's Meagan from her small group at church.

"Have you heard anything?" Meagan asks anxiously.

"They're supposed to let us know tomorrow," Natalie replies.

Last month, the plant announced there would be cutbacks followed by large-scale layoffs.

"Are you worried?"

"I'm trying not to be," Natalie says, "but it's hard. I'm not sleeping a whole lot and I'm biting my nails again. Guess I'm a little stressed."

"Are you and Joy okay?" Meagan asks. "Do you have enough to get by?"

"Yeah, for the most part," Natalie responds. "We're doing the best we can." The two friends chat for a while, pray together, promise to check in the next day, and then hang up.

It's nearly midnight before Natalie finishes paying the bills. As usual, it's a tight race to the finish line, income barely beating out expenses. It's hard, as a single mom, to make ends meet, but the Lord has once again provided. Natalie proudly writes a modest tithe check to her church. "Thank you, Lord!" she exclaims as she closes the checkbook.

As she crawls into bed, Natalie notices the Bible on the nightstand. Her pastor recently challenged everyone at church to read through the Bible in a year. At first, she was very excited, having never read the entire Bible. But the more she got into it, the harder it became. Recent meetings and programs at her daughter's school put her a week behind in her reading, so she's been trying to catch up. She's always struggled with having regular devotions, so Natalie feels guilty and discouraged. She starts getting down on herself for what she's convinced is a lack of discipline. She starts to read, but her eyes grow heavy. Before long, she falls asleep without finishing her Bible-reading assignment.

Discussion Questions

1 Do you know many people who, like Natalie, are tired and overworked?

2 Based on the information provided, do you agree with Natalie's self-assessment that she lacks discipline? Why or why not?

3 What are some of the things Natalie is doing right in her life?

4 What do you think of when you hear the words "devotions," "quiet times," or "spiritual disciplines"?

5 What advice would you give to busy, hard-working people who sincerely desire to practice spiritual disciplines but have limited time?

A Well-Practiced Habit

David observed a regular routine of private worship. According to Psalm 145:2, he worshiped God daily: "Every day I will bless you and praise your name forever and ever." For David, worship was not confined to a weekly Sabbath ritual conducted exclusively at the local synagogue, but was a well-practiced personal habit. Indeed, David intentionally stopped at various times throughout the day to worship God. He wrote, "I will sing aloud of your steadfast love in the morning" (Psalm 59:16). "By day the LORD commands his steadfast love, and at night his song is with me" (Psalm 42:8). In Psalm 57:7–8, he cried out, "I will sing and make melody! Awake, my glory! Awake, O harp and lyre! I will awake the dawn!" Daily private worship was part of David's regular routine. From early morning to late at night, he was quick to praise God. Therefore, David lived a life of continuous worship and invites us to do the same: "May those who love your salvation say continually, 'Great is the LORD!'" (Psalm 40:16).

Stop and Drop

The ancient Jews had fixed hours set aside for prayer and worship. Along with David, Scripture reveals several examples of those who routinely stopped at appointed times during their day to worship God. Daniel, for example, "got down on his knees three times a day and prayed and gave thanks before his God, as he had done previously" (Daniel 6:10). The author of Psalm 119 admits, "Seven times a day I praise you for your righteous rules" (Psalm 119:164). Yet another psalmist exclaims, "It is good to give thanks to the LORD, to sing praises to your name, O Most High; to declare your steadfast love in the morning, and your faithfulness by night" (Psalm 92:1–2).

Praising God regularly produces a worshipful mindset throughout the day. Psalm 113:3 proclaims, "From the rising of the sun to its setting, the name of the LORD is to be praised!" Another ancient songwriter wrote, "My mouth is filled with your praise, and with your glory all the day" (Psalm 71:8). The writer of Hebrews instructs us to "continually offer up a sacrifice of praise to God" (Hebrews 13:15). A life of continual worship is the mark of a true worshiper.

I have the privilege of leading worship for the Transforming Center, a ministry whose mission is to care for the souls of pastors, worship leaders, and lay leaders. At each of our retreats, we "pray the hours." Four times a day, at set times, we gather for prayer and worship, establishing a daily rhythm that breathes life into the soul. Afterward, many who fill out evaluations list those set prayer times as their favorite part of the retreat.

The following suggestions offer some practical ideas on how to worship God privately. Experiment with each practice, especially any that are new to you. You can choose the ones you find most helpful and adapt them to your own needs. Or you may decide to practice all of these disciplines at different times or in varying degrees.

TAKEAWAY #2:

Establish a Regular Routine for Private Worship

It's easier to pray the hours when on a retreat than in real life. Even if we wanted to, most of us don't enjoy the luxury of being able to stop whatever we're doing three or four times a day to worship. However, there are still plenty of worship practices and habits we can build into our daily routines.

Before proceeding, I should offer a few caveats. First, I'm not suggesting you necessarily replace your set routine with the ideas below, but instead incorporate these into your usual practice. Whenever my devotions feel stale, I find that introducing more worship into my routine breathes new life into my quiet times. Second, don't work hard at any of the following practices. The goal is not to spend long hours strenuously laboring to worship God, but to make some form of private worship a regular habit — daily, if possible. To that end, the following suggestions are simple in their approach and flexible as to length; they can be as long or as brief as you like. Busy people, as well as those who struggle to have regular devotions, should find them very doable.

In this chapter I'll be sharing several examples from my own private worship times. Rest assured that I am still learning and growing, that I have a heart for worship, but that I too am on the journey and far from having arrived. I'm always uncomfortable talking about myself for fear of coming across as pretentious. I hope that examples from my own experience prove to be not distracting but helpful in further illustrating each of the following practices for private worship.

ACTS

When I became a Christian, I learned a popular method for prayer that was patterned around the acronym ACTS, which stands for adoration, confession, thanksgiving, and supplication. The first part of that sequence taught me, more than anything else, how to worship God privately. At the beginning of my devotions, I'd spend a few minutes praising God, either verbally or in writing, drawing on whatever attribute of his came to mind. Most often it was one I had recently witnessed or experienced. For example, if I received any kind of blessing, it was easy to praise God for his grace and love. Answered prayer elicited praise for God's faithful-ness. Holidays brought out even more of God's notable qualities. At Christmas, I worshiped Christ as Prince of Peace, Wonderful Counselor, Light of the World, and Emmanuel. During the Easter season, I was drawn to Christ as Savior, Redeemer, and Risen Lord.

I know people who sing their favorite hymns and praise cho-ruses or make up their own songs during their times of adoration. Others write names or attributes of God on little note cards or sticky notes and scatter them around home and/or office. (For a brief list of God's names and attributes, see Appendixes A and B.) Using ACTS is an easy way to instill more worship into your life.

Read a Psalm a Day

Following my initial attempts at private worship, I began read-ing a psalm a day, which I still do today. While reading, I stop at any word or phrase that resonates with me (a name or attribute of God), and I'll use that as a springboard for worship. Psalm 106:1, for example, prompts me to praise God for his goodness and steadfast love: "Praise the LORD! Oh give thanks to the LORD, for he is good, for his steadfast love endures forever!" After read-ing Psalm 66:19, I was eager to praise God for being attentive to prayer: "But truly God has listened; he has attended to the voice of my prayer."

Sometimes the characteristic of God to which I am drawn reflects a specific need in my life. One time, while facing a dif-ficult decision, utterly confused and in desperate need of discern-ment, I happened upon Psalm 16:7 where David says, "I bless the LORD who gives me counsel." So, following David's example, I worshiped God for his infinite wisdom and understanding.

Reading a psalm a day has increased my appreciation for all of God's attributes, not just the ones to which I am attracted. If left to my own devices, I lean more toward the "feel good" attributes like God's mercy, compassion, love, and grace. The psalms rightly point out that God is also holy and just (Psalm 97:2), and that he hates sin and violence (Psalm 11:5). Recently, after listening to the evening news, I was worked up about all the evil and destruction in the world. The next day, I read, "God is a righteous judge, and a God who feels indignation every day" (Psalm 7:11). So I worshiped God as Righteous Judge and drew strength from the fact that he feels even more indignant about violence, poverty, and injustice than we do.

As you can imagine, the Psalms can expand our concept of God, giving us more attributes for which to praise him. The morning I read Psalm 102, I was excited to worship the Lord as Eternal God. "But you, O LORD, are enthroned forever.... Your years have no end" (Psalm 102:12, 27). Unless I happened to be reading a book on theology that day, I probably wouldn't have thought to worship God for his eternal nature. However, the Psalms directed me, as they often do, to a more transcendent view of God.

The Psalter also offers fresh phrases and expressions with which to worship. Sometimes when I'm at a loss for words, I let a psalm speak for me. I simply read out loud a section like Psalm 66:1 – 5:

> Shout for joy to God, all the earth; sing the glory of his name; give to him glorious praise! Say to God, "How awesome are your deeds! So great is your power that your enemies come cringing to you. All the earth worships you and sings praises to you; they sing praises to your name." Come and see what God has done: he is awesome in his deeds toward the children of man.

Psalm 100 is another little gem that's guaranteed to get your worship juices flowing:

Make a joyful noise to the LORD, all the earth! Serve the LORD with gladness! Come into his presence with singing! Know that the LORD, he is God! It is he who made us, and we are his; we are his people, and the sheep of his pasture. Enter his gates with thanksgiving, and his courts with praise! Give thanks to him; bless his name! For the Lord is good; his steadfast love endures forever, and his faithfulness to all generations.

If you're wondering which psalms to read, you could simply start with the beginning and read them in order. Or you could follow a devotional book, lectionary, or Bible reading plan that offers a systematic schedule for reading the psalms daily.

I also recommend that you read psalms aloud, even during private worship. Originally, psalms were intended to be sung or spoken. I find that reading psalms out loud forces me to slow down and read the words more carefully and thoughtfully.

Ask "Who Is God?"

A few years ago, I discipled a young man who, in our first meeting, announced with great passion that he wanted, more than anything else, to know God. So for a full year, I assigned various Bible verses for my young friend to read with two questions in mind:

1. How does this passage apply to my life?
2. What does this Scripture tell me about who God is? This question has since worked its way into my own routine and ignited my private worship.

The Bible is our ultimate authority on God—what he's like, how he thinks, and how he acts. In addition to obvious references to the names and attributes of God, Scripture contains numerous stories, parables, and teachings that provide insight into God's character. Many Christians turn immediately to the Psalms when it's time to worship. However, you could open your Bible to any page, get a glimpse of who God is, and find ample reason to praise him. Let's examine two sections of Scripture that offer plenty of incentive to worship: the Gospels and the Epistles.

The Gospels

Most people read the Gospels for information about Jesus and his teaching. Why not read Matthew, Mark, Luke, and John with an eye toward worship? Throughout the Gospels, God is revealed through his Son, Jesus Christ. When you look at Christ, you're looking at God (2 Corinthians 4:6). Hebrews 1:3 reveals that Christ is "the radiance of the glory of God and the exact imprint of his nature." Jesus said, "Whoever has seen me has seen the Father" (John 14:9). So if you want to know how God interacts with human beings or how God relates to you personally, notice how Jesus talked and ministered to people.

The Gospels, therefore, are replete with God's attributes gloriously revealed and lived out in the person of Jesus Christ. I can't help but notice, for example, how much compassion Christ demonstrated toward ordinary human beings. As he looked out on the crowds of people who came for teaching and healing, Jesus "had compassion for them, because they were harassed and helpless, like sheep without a shepherd" (Matthew 9:36). One time, after several days of intense teaching and ministry, Jesus grew concerned about the people, pulled his disciples aside and said, "I have compassion on the crowd because they have been with me now three days and have nothing to eat" (Matthew 15:32). It wasn't just large crowds that drew Jesus' sympathy, but individuals as well. Jesus felt compassion for a widow whose son died

(Luke 7:13). And when his friend Lazarus died, Scripture reports that Jesus was "deeply moved in his spirit and greatly troubled" to the point of weeping (John 11:33, 35). God holds deep compassion toward anyone who has lost a loved one. After all, his only Son was crucified on a cross for our sins.

Worship is an appropriate response whenever we encounter Christ in the Gospels. Many who witnessed Christ's miracles and healing power responded by glorifying God (Matthew 9:8; 15:31; Luke 5:25–26; 7:16; 13:13). Praise him as the Forgiver of Our Sins (Matthew 9:6; 26:28), Giver of Eternal Life (John 5:21; 17:2), Our Living Bread (John 6:51), Most High God (Mark 5:7), the Way, the Truth, and the Life (John 14:6), Teacher and Lord (John 13:13), and the Light of the World (John 8:12).

Whenever reading the Gospels, be on the lookout for attributes of God exhibited through Jesus Christ. Ask yourself whether the passage before you uncovers any insight about who God is, and then worship accordingly.

The Epistles

Along with the Gospels, as well as the books of Acts and Revelation, the Epistles make up the remainder of the New Testament. Like the rest of Scripture, these letters also contain numerous names, attributes, and descriptions of God. Second Corinthians 1:3 reveals that our God is a "God of all comfort." God is also our provider (Philippians 4:19). First Corinthians 1:24 refers to Christ as "the power of God and the wisdom of God."

Of special interest to worshipers are passages scattered throughout the Epistles that scholars believe to be fragments of first-century hymns:

> Awake, O sleeper, and arise from the dead, and Christ will shine on you.
>
> EPHESIANS 5:14

[Jesus] was manifested in the flesh, vindicated by the Spirit, seen by angels, proclaimed among the nations, believed on in the world, taken up in glory.

1 TIMOTHY 3:16

[Christ Jesus] who, though he was in the form of God, did not count equality with God a thing to be grasped, but made himself nothing, taking the form of a servant, being born in the likeness of men. And being found in human form, he humbled himself by becoming obedient to the point of death, even death on a cross. Therefore God has highly exalted him and bestowed on him the name that is above every name, so that at the name of Jesus every knee should bow, in heaven and on earth and under the earth, and every tongue confess that Jesus Christ is Lord, to the glory of God the Father.

PHILIPPIANS 2:6–11

He is the image of the invisible God, the firstborn of all creation. For by him all things were created, in heaven and on earth, visible and invisible, whether thrones or dominions or rulers or authorities—all things were created through him and for him. And he is before all things, and in him all things hold together. And he is the head of the body, the church. He is the beginning, the firstborn from the dead, that in everything he might be preeminent. For in him all the fullness of God was pleased to dwell, and through him to reconcile to himself all things, whether on earth or in heaven, making peace by the blood of his cross.

COLOSSIANS 1:15–20

The dominant theme in these early hymns of the church is that Christ is preeminent, the glorious image of God, and worthy of our highest praise.

If you want to grow in your knowledge and understanding of

God, read his Word. Whether you're leafing through the Old or New Testament, keep asking, "What does this particular passage tell me about who God is?" Then as you discover or are reminded of who God is—as he reveals himself to you through Scripture —worship him wholeheartedly.

Meditate on the Names and Attributes of God

Scripture informs us that meditating on the attributes of God moved David to worship. "My mouth will praise you with joyful lips, when I remember you upon my bed, and meditate on you in the watches of the night" (Psalm 63:5–6). Another psalmist put the invitation from God quite simply: "Be still, and know that I am God" (Psalm 46:10).

David not only meditated on who God is but also on what God has done. In Psalm 145:5, he wrote these words in praise to his Lord: "On the glorious splendor of your majesty, and on your wondrous works, I will meditate." The other psalmists concur: "I will ponder all your work, and meditate on your mighty deeds" (Psalm 77:12). "Great are the works of the LORD, studied by all who delight in them" (Psalm 111:2).

Taking our cue from David and his fellow songwriters, we too can make meditation a significant part of our private worship. Unfortunately, some people are intimidated by meditation. They've been led to believe that meditation involves sitting in unbearably uncomfortable positions and chanting gibberish for hours on end. Second Timothy 2:7 provides a much simpler definition of meditation. Paul simply advises, "Think over what I say, for the Lord will give you understanding in everything." Christian meditation, as it relates to worship, is simply taking the time to think about who God is and what God has done.

As you read the Psalms, you may notice the Hebrew word *Selah* scattered here and there, mostly at the ends of phrases. Scholars aren't sure exactly what the word means, but most agree that it indicates a musical interlude whereby people are encouraged to think about what they just heard or read. For example, in Psalm 4, "Selah" appears after the second verse, perhaps prompting us to contemplate "vain words" and "lies"—the empty things we pursue, the lies we listen to, or any deceitfulness in our hearts. Verse four reads, "Be angry, and do not sin; ponder in your own hearts on your beds, and be silent." Then David inserts "Selah" as if to say, "Hey, don't read any further. Think about what I just said." So the invitation to meditate appears throughout psalmody.

To meditate worshipfully, start with a specific name or attribute of God revealed in the Bible and then ponder its significance in your life. Allow the Holy Spirit to guide your thoughts, but if it helps, consider the following questions:

> How have I seen this particular name or attribute of God manifested in my life or in the world around me?
>
> Why am I drawn to this particular aspect of God's character?
>
> How did Jesus embody this attribute of God?
>
> How can I reflect this part of God to others?
>
> Is God inviting me to do anything in relation to this particular name or attribute?

Psalm 31:19, for example, led me to worship the Lord for his infinite goodness. But I also couldn't help but think about God's goodness to me. In my journal I listed as many examples as I could think of.

If you want to take your worship to a deeper level, try meditating on the character of God.

Pray the Names
and Attributes of God

When Jesus taught his disciples to pray, he began with worship: "Our Father in heaven, hallowed be your name" (Matthew 6:9). The Lord's Prayer traditionally ends with worship as well: "For yours is the kingdom and the power and the glory, forever. Amen."

Many of David's psalms are prayers that are laced with worship. In Psalm 86:8–10, sandwiched between several urgent prayer requests, David extols the supremacy of God:

> There is none like you among the gods, O Lord, nor are there any works like yours. All the nations you have made shall come and worship before you, O Lord, and shall glorify your name. For you are great and do wondrous things; you alone are God.

According to David, prayer and praise go together; you can't have one without the other. The great eighteenth-century Anglican priest William Law agrees:

> When you begin your petitions, use such various expressions of the attributes of God as may make you most sensible of the greatness and power of the Divine Nature.
>
> Begin, therefore, in words like these: O Being of all beings, Fountain of all light and glory, gracious Father of men and Angels, whose universal Spirit is everywhere present, giving life, and light, and joy to all Angels in Heaven, and all creatures upon earth, etc.
>
> For these representations of the Divine attributes, which show us in some degree the Majesty and greatness of God, are an excellent means of raising our hearts into lively acts of worship and adoration.[13]

Worship-based prayer involves praying through the names or

attributes of God. Therefore, it is prayer that emerges from, or as a result of, worship. Recently, as I read about Jesus calming the storm (Mark 4:35–41), I praised him as the only source of true peace, thought of all the storms swirling in my own life at the time, and asked Christ to calm each and every one of them.

Worshiping God as Redeemer or Savior usually compels me to pray for friends and relatives who don't yet know Christ. Psalm 146:9 persuades me not only to worship God as the one who "upholds the widow and the fatherless" but also to pray for all the single moms I know as well as their kids.

Do you ever feel like your prayers are dull and repetitive? I often feel that way about mealtime prayers—that I keep saying the same thing over and over. For that reason, I've been trying to include a line or two of praise for an attribute of God when I say grace. If you want to breathe more life into your prayers, try praying as you worship and worshiping as you pray.

Daily Praise Offering

For several years, I've been practicing a spiritual discipline I call my "Daily Praise Offering." As I go through Psalms and other Bible readings, I look for something I can offer the Lord as a personal expression of worship. Usually it's a name or attribute of God for which I praise him. But it can also be an entire verse or short phrase of Scripture that I proclaim out loud to the Lord. After practicing this routine for a couple months, I noticed that my little expression of worship or that attribute of God would become a running theme throughout my day.

Yesterday, for example, after reading Psalm 89, I wrote this line in my journal based on verse 7: "Lord, I stand in awe of you for you are awesome above all." Throughout the day, that line came to mind as I prayed before meals, spoke with friends, and drove around town. In other words, God's awesomeness became the theme of my day, much like David describes in Psalm 44:8 when he says, "In God we have boasted continually." All day yesterday, I enjoyed bragging about how awesome God is.[14]

On other occasions, my "Daily Praise Offering" has helped me get through challenging and difficult times. One morning, for example, I awakened from a restless night of sleep with a long day of stressful meetings ahead and an urgent writing deadline to boot. While reading Psalm 28, I was immediately drawn to verse 7: "The Lord is my strength and my shield; in him my heart trusts, and I am helped." It's no coincidence that God's strength emerged as my chosen attribute for that particular day; I was in desperate need of his power in my life. What could have been a nerve-racking day turned out to be one of great peace and productivity. I was reminded several times to worship God and draw upon his strength, even during the tense moments of my workday.

If a "Daily Praise Offering" is too ambitious for now, make it a "Weekly Praise Offering" if that's more feasible. I've also gotten into the habit of identifying an attribute of God for the year. This past year, for example, has been very challenging for me personally. Ministry has been overwhelming at times, my mother passed away, my wife, Sue, went through depression, and a close relative vehemently rejected Sue and me, saying he didn't want to have anything to do with us ever again because we're Christians. It's been a dark night for this weary soul. At one point, I happened upon Romans 15:4–5: "For whatever was written in former days was written for our instruction, that through endurance and through the encouragement of the Scriptures we might have hope. May the God of endurance and encouragement grant you to live in such harmony with one another, in accord with Christ Jesus." This passage touched me on such a deep level because I desperately needed strength to endure and hungered for any word of encouragement I could get. Many times this year I have worshiped the "God of endurance and encouragement" and, in the process, discovered him to be just that.

However you choose to practice it, adopting a specific attribute of God as your theme for the day, week, or year is guaranteed to enhance your worship.

Write Your Own Psalm

Some of you may want to write your own psalm—express worship in your own words. Your original psalm doesn't have to be wordy or eloquent; it doesn't even have to rhyme. It just has to be an honest and concise articulation of your thoughts or feelings to God. Those of you who enjoy being creative might want to set your psalm to music, write a poem, dance, or paint a picture. Whatever means you choose, this "do-it-yourself" approach can greatly enrich your private worship experience.

The biblical psalms can be roughly divided into three very basic categories: songs of lament, hymns of thanksgiving, and hymns of praise. Should you elect to compose your own psalm, keep in mind these simple guidelines.

Hymns of Thanksgiving

Hymns of thanksgiving express gratitude for who God is and/or something God has done in the life of the writer. A thanksgiving psalm refers to a specific experience and gives witness to how God intervened. So the overall tone is joyful, with a deep awareness of God's unmerited favor and blessing. Psalms 9 and 30 are good examples of thanksgiving hymns, as are salvation testimonies and stories about answered prayer. Characteristically, hymns of thanksgiving include three factors:

- They describe a past problem.
- They recount how God intervened.
- They express thanksgiving for God's grace.

Hymns of Praise

Hymns of praise call God's people to respect, admire, and revere God's attributes and mighty deeds. They may not refer to a specific experience because hymns of praise begin with the premise that God is worthy of praise simply because he is God. As a result, such psalms highlight various names or attributes of God. Psalms 8, 93, and 145 are perfect examples. Thus, hymns of praise follow three principles:

- Generally start by calling God's people to worship
- State specific reasons to worship God
- Cite specific names or attributes of God

Songs of Lament

Songs of lament are expressions of deep grief, anger, or sorrow related to personal hardship and crisis. They reflect an honest struggle to make sense of the pain of this world. Amid great adversity, the writer turns to God, knowing that God is the only one who can rescue, vindicate, and make things right. Songs of lament typically move from desperation to hope. Examples include Psalms 12 and 13. In writing a song of lament, keep in mind the following guidelines. Generally, songs of lament include three statements:

- They are addressed to God.
- They state a personal problem or crisis.
- They eventually affirm hope and trust in God.

As you pen your own psalm, please remember that you don't have to produce a literary masterpiece for God to accept your worship. Unless you decide to share your psalm with others, it can always remain between you and God.

What Helps You Experience God's Greatness?

Most people can identify one or two activities that pull them quickly and easily into worship. Make sure you include such activities regularly in your routine—schedule them if necessary —to allow for more worship in your life. Let's briefly examine two common examples—listening to worship music and being out in nature—and discuss how each can trigger private worship.

Worship Music

For many people, nothing else moves them to worship as effectively as music. David was a musician; he played the harp (1 Samuel 16:14–23), he sang (Psalm 7:17), and he was known as the "sweet psalmist of Israel" (2 Samuel 23:1). Indeed, music is a marvelous gift from God. Being a musician myself, I often end my devotions by picking up my guitar and singing praise to the Lord. However, you don't have to be a musician to incorporate and enjoy worship music. Hymns and praise choruses are readily available for private, as well as corporate, worship.

For hundreds of years, the great hymns of the faith have been a valuable resource for worship. A. W. Tozer, a zealous advocate for the use of hymns in private worship, wrote passionately:

> If you were to go to my study, you would discover piles of hymnbooks. As a singer, I leave a lot to be desired; but that is nobody's business. My singing is an expression of my wor-

ship of the Almighty God above. God listens while I sing to Him old French hymns and translations of the old Latin hymns and old Greek hymns from the Eastern Church; and of course, the beautiful songs done in meter as well as some of the simpler songs of Watts and Wesley and the rest. The Christian hymnal is a beautiful place to begin a daily regimen of worshiping God.[15]

I know a couple who select a different hymn every week, check out a recording of it from the library or download it off the Internet, and listen to it as part of their Sabbath observance.

A hymn title alone can serve as a springboard for worship. Recently, I read Psalm 90 in which Moses describes some of the glorious activities of God on behalf of the nation of Israel. I was having difficulty summarizing an appropriate attribute of God until I realized that the hymn "O God, Our Help in Ages Past" is based on this psalm. On many occasions, I've appropriated the title of a hymn or praise chorus as my "Daily Praise Offering."

It's easy to find recordings of your favorite worship songs these days. Many people play worship CDs as they drive, work, or even exercise. Some prefer to listen to praise music on their way to church. Psalms 120–134 are commonly known as the "Songs of Ascent." They were recited or sung by ancient worshipers as they journeyed to Jerusalem for religious pilgrimage and/or climbed the steps of the temple. The purpose of these psalms was to prepare the people's hearts for worship. In the same way, listening to worship music before church can help you get ready to worship. Sing along. Read the lyrics. Meditate on the words. Pray them. Look up related Bible verses. Write down any thoughts you have in response. If you're a fan of worship music, I challenge you to include it as part of your private worship.

Nature

Being a shepherd, David spent a lot of time outdoors. As a result, he was constantly in awe of God's creation. He saw God as . . .

> the hope of all the ends of the earth and of the farthest seas; the one who by his strength established the mountains, being girded with might; who stills the roaring of the seas, the roaring of their waves, the tumult of the peoples, so that those who dwell at the ends of the earth are in awe at your signs.
>
> PSALM 65:5–8

It's easy to imagine young David, perched on a rock along a hill outside Bethlehem, singing, "For the LORD is a great God, and a great King above all gods. In his hand are the depths of the earth; the heights of the mountains are his also. The sea is his, for he made it, and his hands formed the dry land" (Psalm 95:3–5).

Like David, many of us stand in awe of creation. We stop at scenic overlooks or get up early to watch the sunrise, beckoned by beauty. I, for one, love to hike. When surrounded by green grass and blue sky, it's easy for me to worship. Being in the mountains or near water rejuvenates and inspires me.

If you're a nature lover, you need to schedule regular field trips to the nearest forest preserve, nature center, or beach. You could go for long leisurely walks every day or once a week. Consider a bike ride or road trip into the country. Bring a camera and take pictures. Draw or sketch your favorite scenes. Write down your thoughts. Describe what you see. Read Scripture. And don't forget to worship as you go. Sing praise to the Lord. May you join David, a fellow nature lover, in exclaiming, "The heavens declare the glory of God, and the sky above proclaims his handiwork" (Psalm 19:1).

Whether it's listening to music, being out in nature, or doing something else that calls forth your worship, make sure you intentionally incorporate those activities into your regular routine. And as you practice the suggestions outlined in this chapter, may the Lord lead you ever deeper in the exciting spiritual discipline of private worship.

Ponder and Apply

1 Which of the practices for private worship described in this chapter seems most inviting to you?

2 Do you currently have a set routine for private worship? If so, is there anything you can do to deepen the experience?

3 If you don't currently practice private worship, how can you incorporate this spiritual discipline into your regular routine?

4 Choose one of the worship ideas discussed and practice it for a week. Report back to your small group, friend, or accountability partner about its effect on you personally.

5 Is there an attribute of God that stands out as a theme for you over the past year?

FOR PASTORS AND WORSHIP LEADERS

I have no doubt that my pastor is a private worshiper. He knows more praise songs than the average worship leader and, on occasion, will sit at his piano at home and worship the Lord one-on-one. Several times, I've heard him share poignant moments he's experienced in private worship. On Sundays, he can be seen in the front row, singing with his arms raised in worship. When it comes to private worship, Pastor James leads by example.

In ancient Israel, the spiritual leaders were avid worshipers. In 1 Chronicles 23:30, we learn that the Levites were instructed to "stand every morning, thanking and praising the LORD, and likewise at evening." Leaders need to model what it means to be a private worshiper.

CHAPTER 3

I Surrender All
Smash Your Idols

Photographs never tell the whole story. Wedding pictures can't tell us how a couple met, where they went on their first date, or how their song became "their song." No one knows that better than Debbie. Curled up on the couch, with an afghan over her lap, Debbie picks up her wedding album. There she is in all her bridal glory, ravishingly pretty and flanked by a beautiful bevy of beaming bridesmaids—her best friends. She's lost track of a couple of her old pals, but is still very close to the others.

Debbie had dreamed of her wedding day since she was a little girl. However, dreams rarely play out according to plan. She pictured everything: the dress, the church, the triple-tier cake, the stained-glass windows, and the velvet red runner stretching to the altar. She imagined walking elegantly down the aisle to a full orchestra playing "Here Comes the Bride," and the man of her dreams—tall, dark, and handsome—waiting in rapture at the other end. Instead, Debbie got married in a banquet hall and waltzed down the aisle to that '90s hit "Everything I Do, I Do It for You" sung by her cousin Beth. But the ceremony was still beautiful in its simplicity and the groom was definitely tall, dark, handsome, and hopelessly enraptured.

Debbie met Mike at work. They started dating and hit it off immediately. At first, Debbie was hesitant about Mike. Debbie is a Christian; Mike, by his own admission, is not. Her friends warned Debbie against dating a non-Christian and shared Bible verses along with their concern, but Debbie's emotions were escalating. "He may not be a Christian yet," she told her friends, "but he's a good man. He loves me and treats me well."

A month later, Mike and Debbie had their first fight, and she saw a side of her new boyfriend she had never seen before. Mike had a bad temper. He was not physically abusive, but he yelled and belittled her. Debbie broke off the relationship. Two days later Mike came to Debbie in tears and apologized. She took him back.

Six weeks later, Mike proposed. Debbie didn't know what to say. She felt conflicted and told Mike she needed to pray about it for a few days. All her Christian friends continued to warn Debbie against marrying a non-believer, but she was no longer listening.

Meanwhile, Mike started attending Debbie's church, and everything she felt for him came rushing back. *He's such a nice guy, she thought, and I'm not getting any younger. I know what the Bible says, but my biological clock is ticking and I can't stand the thought of being alone the rest of my life. More than anything else in the world, I want to get married. After all, God wants me to be happy, doesn't he?*

That summer, Debbie got what she wanted. She and Mike were married on a bright sunny afternoon in June. She has the pictures to prove it. But now, as she stares at the giddy bride smiling back at her, it's all a distant memory.

Debbie sighs as she closes the wedding album and slams it into a hefty black garbage bag. She's keeping the pictures of her and her bridesmaids, but throwing out all the pictures of Mike. She ties up the bag, carries it outside, and sets it along the curb. She pauses momentarily in the moonlight but can't bring herself to cry; there are no more tears left.

After they got married, Mike stopped going to church. His outbursts grew more volatile. Debbie began seeing things that she hadn't noticed before, including his blatant selfishness and wandering eye. But it was his lying and cheating that shattered her trust and broke her spirit. They fought a lot. Within two years, they were divorced.

It just goes to show that photographs don't tell the whole story … especially wedding pictures.

Discussion Questions

1 What factors contributed to the failure of Mike and Debbie's marriage?

2 How would you have counseled Debbie after Mike proposed?

3 Why did Debbie not listen to the advice of her Christian friends or heed the warnings of Scripture?

4 What did Debbie want more than anything and why?

5 Do you think Debbie wanted a husband more than she wanted the Lord? Why, or why not?

The Highest Form of Worship

David regarded obedience as the highest form of worship: "In sacrifice and offering you have not delighted.… Burnt offering and sin offering you have not required.… I delight to do your will, O my God; your law is within my heart" (Psalm 40:6–8). David loved God's Word, treasured it in his heart, and strived to obey it.

In fact, the reason God referred to David as a "man after his own heart" was because David, though far from perfect, was serious about doing God's will (1 Samuel 13:14). God said, "I have found in David the son of Jesse a man after my heart, who will do all my will" (Acts 13:22). For David, obedience was an expression of worship. He held that God "leads me in paths of righteousness for his name's sake" (Psalm 23:3).

Worship and obedience go hand in hand. In Psalm 5, for example, amid heartfelt worship, David affirms his desire to live a life of obedience to God: "I will bow down toward your holy temple in the fear of you. Lead me, O LORD, in your righteousness" (Psalm 5:7–8).

It is no surprise that one of David's goals was to be a man of integrity: "I will walk with integrity of heart within my house; I will not set before my eyes anything that is worthless" (Psalm 101:2–3). In Psalm 141:4, David earnestly prayed, "Do not let my heart incline to any evil, to busy myself with wicked deeds." In fact, David penned an entire song stressing the importance of godliness in the life of the worshiper. Here's how it begins:

> O LORD, who shall sojourn in your tent? Who shall dwell on your holy hill? He who walks blamelessly and does what is right and speaks truth in his heart; who does not slander with his tongue and does no evil to his neighbor, nor takes up a reproach against his friend.
>
> PSALM 15:1–3

Those close to David knew him to be a man of virtue. Solomon described his father as a man who walked before God in "faithfulness, in righteousness, and in uprightness of heart" (1 Kings 3:6). Asaph, a fellow hymn writer, spoke admiringly of David's leadership over Israel, saying, "With upright heart he shepherded them and guided them with his skillful hand" (Psalm 78:72). Serious worshipers strive to be people of godly character and integrity.

Jesus also equated obedience with worship. He said, "If you love me, you will keep my commandments. Whoever has my commandments and keeps them, he it is who loves me" (John 14:15, 21). You can't express love to Jesus and then ignore his will, do whatever you want, and break his commandments.

Willful disobedience renders our worship unacceptable to God. In the book of Amos, God vehemently rejects worship from the people of Israel because of their superficiality and their selfish disregard for the poor and oppressed.

> I hate, I despise your feasts, and I take no delight in your solemn assemblies. Even though you offer me your burnt offerings and grain offerings, I will not accept them; and the peace offerings of your fattened animals, I will not look upon them. Take away from me the noise of your songs; to the melody of your harps I will not listen. But let justice roll down like waters, and righteousness like an ever-flowing stream.
>
> AMOS 5:21–24

When what we sing doesn't match what we do, the result is hypocritical worship, which is something that God absolutely loathes.

The Opposite of Worship

Sin is a refusal to glorify God. The Bible bluntly chastises those of us who know God but don't honor him as God (Romans 1:21). R. C. Sproul refers to such blasphemy as "treason against the divine glory."[16]

Indeed, sin is to be taken seriously. A. W. Tozer reminds us that "God hates sin because He is a holy God. He knows that sin has filled the world with pain and sorrow, robbing us of our principal purpose and joy in life, the joy of worshiping our God!"[17]

Commenting on Romans 3:23, which states that "all have sinned and fall short of the glory of God," John Piper explains:

> Sinning is a "falling short" of the glory of God. But the Greek for "falling short" (*husterountai*) means "lack." The idea is not that you shot an arrow at God's glory and the arrow fell short, but that you could have had it as a treasure, but you don't. You have chosen something else instead.... That is the deepest problem with sin: it is a suicidal exchange of infinite value and beauty for some fleeting, inferior substitute.[18]

Paul speaks of those who foolishly "exchanged the glory of the immortal God for images resembling mortal man and birds and animals and creeping things.... They exchanged the truth about God for a lie and worshiped and served the creature rather than the Creator" (Romans 1:23, 25; see also Psalm 106:20). Every time we disobey, we replace God and his glory with some "inferior substitute," which amounts to idolatry.

Modern-Day Idolatry

All the talk about idolatry in the Bible seemed antiquated when I first became a Christian. I couldn't imagine any of my neighbors actually bowing down before a golden calf or any other fancy statue. I now realize that idolatry runs rampant in our world today. But even worse is the idolatry lurking in my own heart.

What Is Idolatry?

A. W. Tozer contends that "idolatry is simply worship directed in any direction but God's, which is the epitome of blasphemy."[19]

Pastor Timothy Keller, in his excellent book *Counterfeit Gods*, writes:

> [An idol] is anything more important to you than God, anything that absorbs your heart and imagination more than God, anything you seek to give you what only God can give.
>
> A counterfeit god is anything so central and essential to your life that, should you lose it, your life would feel hardly worth living. An idol has such a controlling position in your heart that you can spend most of your passion and energy, your emotional and financial resources, on it without a second thought. It can be family and children, or career and making money, or achievement and critical acclaim, or saving "face" and social standing. It can be a romantic relationship, peer approval, competence and skill, secure and comfortable circumstances, your beauty or your brains, a great political or social cause, your morality and virtue, or even success in the Christian ministry.... An idol is whatever you look at and say, in your heart of hearts, "If I have that, then I'll feel my life has meaning, then I'll know I have value, then I'll feel significant and secure." There are many ways to describe that kind of relationship to something, but perhaps the best one is *worship*.[20]

We all worship something or someone that becomes, for better or worse, a driving force in our lives. The question is whether we're worshiping the one true God or some sorry substitute. Pastor Francis Chan questions why we would ever choose to live for anything other than God:

> We say to the Creator ... "Well, I'm not sure You are worth it.... You see, I really like my car, or my little sin habit, or my money, and I'm really not sure I want to give them up, even if it means I get You."

When we put it plainly like this — as a direct choice between God and our stuff — most of us hope we would choose God. But we need to realize that how we spend our time, what our money goes toward, and where we will invest our energy is equivalent to choosing God or rejecting Him. How could we think for even a second that something on this puny little earth compares to the Creator and Sustainer and Savior of it all?[21]

Idolatry is not only a threat to authentic Christ-centered worship; it is the root cause of all sin and bad behavior. One time a disgruntled sibling tattled on his brother to Jesus. "Teacher, tell my brother to divide the inheritance with me," he complained. Jesus saw straight through the man's posturing to the real issue and said, "Take care, and be on your guard against all covetousness, for one's life does not consist in the abundance of his possessions" (Luke 12:13–15). The underlying problem in this family squabble was idolatry. The embattled brother had put material possessions on a pedestal. Keller writes:

Idolatry is always the reason we ever do anything wrong. No one grasped this better than Martin Luther. In his *Large Catechism* (1529) and in his *Treatise on Good Works* he wrote that the Ten Commandments begin with a commandment against idolatry. Why does this come first? Because, he argued, the fundamental motivation behind lawbreaking is idolatry. We never break the commandments without breaking the first one. Why do we fail to love or keep promises or live unselfishly? Of course, the general answer is "because we are weak and sinful," but the specific answer in any circumstance is that there is something you feel you *must* have to be happy, something that is more important to your heart than God himself.[22]

In our opening scenario, Debbie desperately wanted to get married. Marriage was more than a dream for her; it had become a blinding obsession. She wanted to be married more than she wanted to obey God.

Idols are not necessarily bad in and of themselves. Many of our counterfeit gods are actually good things, which is why we pin our hopes and dreams on them. But even the best things in life can never replace God. Sin, therefore, is not just a matter of doing bad things or breaking God's rules. Sin is letting a good thing become an ultimate thing and, therefore, taking the place of God in our lives.

Serious Affront to God

Idolatry is an insult to God. Deuteronomy 6:14–15 warns, "You shall not go after other gods ... for the LORD your God in your midst is a jealous God—lest the anger of the LORD your God be kindled against you, and he destroy you from off the face of the earth." The Bible is adamant that God alone is worthy of our praise and adoration. "There shall be no strange god among you; you shall not bow down to a foreign god. I am the LORD your God" (Psalm 81:9–10; see also Exodus 34:14; Acts 10:25–26; Revelation 19:10). Believers cannot tolerate idolatry, no matter how subtle or innocuous it may seem. Nothing can or should take the place of God in our lives.

When Satan tempted Jesus in the wilderness, his main objective was to get Christ to fall down and worship Satan. In reply, Jesus quoted Deuteronomy 6:13, "You shall worship the Lord your God and him only shall you serve" (Matthew 4:10). There's no way Jesus would exchange the glory of God for anything Satan could offer.

Idols Lie

Idols are dangerously deceptive. They disrupt rational thinking, distort our feelings, and render us blind to reality. Beware of the hidden lies behind every false god.

They Insist We Need Them

Idols brainwash us into thinking we absolutely need them whatever the cost. That's why we become obsessed with acquiring a bigger house, a new car, or more clothes. Idols try to tell us we're missing out unless we partake. We become convinced that we have to look at that pornographic website, go to that party, get more money, or give in to a boyfriend's demand for sex. We may even be persuaded we have certain needs that justify wrong behavior. Idols tend to establish morality on their own terms, making it plausible for us to "call evil good and good evil" (Isaiah 5:20).

Truth is, we don't need those things we're addicted to or think we've got to have. "For all the gods of the peoples are worthless idols" (Psalm 96:5). When we sin, what we're really missing out on is all that God has for us. Jonah 2:8 reminds us, "Those who pay regard to vain idols forsake their hope of steadfast love." Every time we run after other gods, we forfeit the grace we could have had.

When God confronted David about his affair with Bathsheba, he reminded David of all the blessings he had been given as well as those God would have bestowed had David been faithful. God said, "And if this were too little, I would add to you as much more" (2 Samuel 12:8). I shudder to think of how much of God's blessing I've missed over the years because of my own willful disobedience.

They Promise to Satisfy

Idols promise to satisfy, but always deliver nothing but heartache and pain. David wrote, "The sorrows of those who run after another god shall multiply" (Psalm 16:4). Psalm 97:7 says, "All worshipers of images are put to shame, who make their boast in worthless idols." In Psalm 38, David attests to the folly of sin with agonizing severity:

> There is no health in my bones because of my sin. For my iniquities have gone over my head; like a heavy burden, they are too heavy for me. My wounds stink and fester because of my foolishness, I am utterly bowed down and prostrate; all the day I go about mourning. For my sides are filled with burning, and there is no soundness in my flesh. I am feeble and crushed; I groan because of the tumult of my heart. My heart throbs; my strength fails me, and the light of my eyes —it also has gone from me.
>
> PSALM 38:3–8, 10

Idols are inadequate and inept (Psalm 115:5–8), always leaving us groping for more.

They Claim to Be Harmless

Finally, idols falsely claim to be harmless, but they most assuredly are not. We've all witnessed the consequences of bad moral choices either in our own lives or the lives of others. In describing those caught up in idolatry, Psalm 106:36 says, "They served their idols, which became a snare to them." David offers these sobering words about the long-term consequences of sin: "For my life is spent with sorrow, and my years with sighing; my strength fails because of my iniquity, and my bones waste away" (Psalm 31:10). Idols are alarmingly destructive. Bad choices can ruin your life.

Like my pastor, James MacDonald, says: "Choose to sin, choose to suffer."

Identify Your Idols

Some of you can immediately identify your idols through an unhealthy attraction, self-destructive behavior, or a besetting sin that has become a driving force in your life. You feel "out of control," indulging beyond what you know is right, doing things you really don't want to do or will later regret. Perhaps you find yourself gripped by an addiction or a nefarious obsession.

In other cases, idolatry may be subtle, but just as insidious. To help name any hidden idols, consider the following questions.

1. *What do you most think about?* An idol is anything that dominates your mind or controls your behavior more than the Holy Spirit does. So pay attention to your thoughts. Do you constantly daydream or fantasize about something or someone to the point of obsession? Do you notice any negative or self-centered attitudes? Whatever your mind dwells on rules your life.

2. *How do you spend your money?* Jesus said, "For where your treasure is, there your heart will be also" (Matthew 6:21). Overspending, paying inordinate amounts of money on a particular object or activity, may indicate a vain attempt to buy happiness.

3. *What sets you off emotionally?* What makes you uncontrollably angry? What are you anxious about? What do you fear the most? What keeps you awake at night? Counterfeit gods constantly stir up negative emotions.

4. *What brings you peace, joy, security, or fulfillment?* Is it your job, personal achievement, your talent, financial prosperity, or God?

5. *How do you react when an idol is taken away?* Ultimately, you can tell whether something is an idol by how you respond if it's removed. Even the threat of losing it will trigger despair. If you're devastated and paralyzed, convinced you can't go on without it, or if you bitterly turn away from God, what you lost may have been, to one degree or another, an idol in your life. There's a saying that goes, "We don't realize that Jesus is all we need until Jesus is all we have."

Uncompromising Commitment

I was part of the original youth group that started Willow Creek Community Church back in the 1970s, and I served as the music director at the church for twenty years. So I sat under the teaching of Bill Hybels for over two decades. Some of Bill's most memorable messages challenged us to full commitment to Christ. The mission of Willow was to "turn irreligious people into fully devoted followers of Christ." Bill would say things like, "Ninety percent commitment to Christ is 10 percent short." He exhorted us to be "Just Say the Word" Christians—people who did without question or compromise what Jesus asked them to do, like the faithful centurion in Matthew 8:5 – 13. A line from one of the church's all-time favorite songs reads, "I don't want to be a casual Christian." For us, a "casual Christian" was a contradiction in terms.

Jesus never watered down what it means to follow him. He said, "Whoever loves father or mother more than me is not worthy of me, and whoever loves son or daughter more than me is not worthy of me" (Matthew 10:37). Christ never relaxed or softened the requirements for discipleship: "Whoever does not bear his own cross and come after me cannot be my disciple" (Luke 14:27). "So therefore, any one of you who does not renounce all that he has cannot be my disciple" (Luke 14:33). Jesus wants all of us, and he calls us to a wholehearted, uncompromising, lifelong, and life-altering commitment.

Jesus won't settle for being just another consideration amid all our other stuff. Francis Chan agrees:

> Most of our thoughts are centered on the money we want to make, the school we want to attend, the body we aspire to have, the spouse we want to marry, the kind of person we want to become.... But the fact is that nothing should concern us more than our relationship with God.... God is not someone who can be tacked on to our lives.[23]

Jesus doesn't want us to try to fit him into our agenda. The Christian life doesn't allow for Jesus and my porn habit, or my greed, or my selfish desires to coexist. "No one can serve two masters, for either he will hate the one and love the other, or he will be devoted to the one and despise the other" (Matthew 6:24). Christ deserves to be at the top of the list, the center of our lives, first place in all things. Theologian David Peterson asserts, "Worship in New Testament terms means responding with one's whole life and being to the divine kingship of Jesus."[24] Obedience, therefore, is the essence of true worship.

Are there any idols, any habitual sins, any bad habits standing between you and full commitment to Christ? Are you ready to tell God that he can have all of you? Are you willing to forsake anything in your life that keeps you from following Christ wholeheartedly?

Destruction of Idols

After one of the battles in which David defeated the Philistines, Scripture reports that David ordered all their idols to be burned

---

TAKEAWAY #3:
Smash Your Idols

Colossians 3:5 instructs us to "Put to death … what is earthly in you: sexual immorality, impurity, passion, evil desire, and covetousness, which is idolatry." Explore what it means to put your idols to death, to smash them to bits once and for all.

(1 Chronicles 14:12). About four hundred years later, King Josiah dealt with idolatry in Israel by smashing all the idols associated with pagan worship (2 Chronicles 34:3–4). Both men were following God's prescribed method for dealing with idols as laid out in Deuteronomy 12:3: "You shall tear down their altars and dash in pieces their pillars and burn their Asherim [false gods] with fire. You shall chop down the carved image of their gods and destroy their name out of that place" (see also Exodus 34:13).

Repent Early and Often

Some of us prayed a "prayer of repentance" when we came to Christ and have wrongly concluded that repentance is a one-time deal. The Bible clearly teaches that repentance is to be ongoing. Every time the Holy Spirit convicts of sin, he is inviting us to repent. That's why Martin Luther began his Ninety-Five Theses by stating that all believers are to live a life of repentance.

Repentance is a recurring theme throughout David's psalms. In Psalm 38, he is simply saying, "I confess my iniquity; I am sorry for my sin." David knows that he can't conceal his sin from God. In Psalm 69:5, he prays, "O God, you know my folly; the wrongs I have done are not hidden from you." After his affair with

Bathsheba, David penned Psalm 51, in which he took full responsibility for his sin. He didn't make excuses or blame anyone else. He owned up to the fact that he, of his own volition, offended a holy God. David also pleaded for God to change him. "Create in me a clean heart, O God, and renew a right spirit within me" (Psalm 51:10). A sincere desire to change is a sign of true repentance.

Through the prophet Ezekiel, God implores each of us: "Repent and turn away from your idols" (Ezekiel 14:6). True repentance involves turning away from—and forsaking—sin. Right now, are there any sins or hidden idolatry you need to confess?

Flee Idolatry

Once you've identified your idols, stay clear of them. Don't give them any credence in your thoughts or any room in your heart. Paul says it straight out: "Therefore, my beloved, flee from idolatry" (1 Corinthians 10:14). It is never a good idea to dabble in sin. First John 5:21 says, "Little children, keep yourselves from idols." Likewise, David wrote, "Turn away from evil and do good; seek peace and pursue it" (Psalm 34:14). "Keep back your servant also from presumptuous sins; let them not have dominion over me!" (Psalm 19:13).

Timothy Keller also strongly urges that we flee idolatry:

> We must not make the mistake of thinking that ... all we have to do is be *willing* to part with our idols rather than actually leave them behind.... Something is safe for us to maintain in our lives only if it has really stopped being an idol. That can happen only when we are truly willing to live without it, when we truly say from the heart: "Because I have God, I can live without you."[25]

Jesus said, "Bear fruit in keeping with repentance" (Matthew 3:8). True repentance results in action. Leaving your idols behind is a sure sign of a changed heart.

Repentance and fleeing idolatry bring God glory (Joshua 7:19). Every time we say no to sin, renounce bad habits, or die to selfishness, it is as an act of worship. With that in mind, is there any sin you need to cut off? Any bad habits you need to stop? Are you dabbling in anything that is turning your heart away from God? Ask the Lord to give you the strength to part ways with any idols in your life.

Replace Your Idols

It's not enough to repent and flee idolatry. To really smash an idol or overcome a nagging sin, it's essential to replace it with something better, something more life giving, something from the Lord. For example, in 2 Timothy 2:22, Paul wrote, "So flee youthful passions and pursue righteousness, faith, love, and peace, along with those who call on the Lord from a pure heart." Notice the progression: flee something bad (lust) and replace it with something good (pursuing spiritual things in fellowship with other believers). Galatians 5:16 instructs us to "walk by the Spirit, and you will not gratify the desires of the flesh." The more we yield to the Holy Spirit, the less attractive sin becomes. Similarly, David sang, "Delight yourself in the LORD, and he will give you the desires of your heart" (Psalm 37:4). We are invited to delight in the Lord, to draw near to Christ and fellowship with him. In the context of an intimate relationship with God, he shapes our desires, replacing temporal idols with a hunger for spiritual things.

Cling to the Cross

The cross is a powerful weapon against sin. When facing temptation, I have often prayed, "Jesus, thank you for dying on the cross for me. Help me to remember that I am dead to this sin and alive in you" (see Romans 6:11 – 13).

At other times, the prayer might go something like this: "Jesus, thank you for the cross. You have conquered sin, so render this idol powerless in my life. Give me the strength to say no" (see Romans 6:14).

When feeling pulled into an idol's web, the cross reminds me of what I have in Christ: "Jesus, you died in order to bring me into fellowship with God. What more could I possibly want? I don't need this idol. I have you" (see 2 Corinthians 5:18).

Dismantling an idol or overcoming sin is not a matter of trying harder but living into the reality of what Christ already accomplished on Calvary. There really is power in the blood of the Lamb.

> Would you be free from your burden of sin?
> There's power in the blood, power in the blood.
> Would you over evil a victory win?
> There's wonderful power in the blood.
> There is power, power, wonder-working power
> In the blood of the Lamb.
> There is power, power, wonder-working power
> In the precious blood of the Lamb.[26]

Choose to Worship

Every time we worship, publicly or privately, we are afforded an opportunity to renounce our idols and affirm allegiance to God. With David, we proclaim, "But I trust in you, O Lord; I say, 'You are my God'" (Psalm 31:14). We join Moses, who unequivocally declared, "This is my God, and I will praise him, my father's God, and I will exalt him" (Exodus 15:2). We chime in with the other psalmists who sang, "This is God, our God forever and ever. He will guide us forever" (Psalm 48:14; see also Psalm 118:28).

When we worship, we proclaim our freedom from idolatry; we turn our backs on worldly possessions, affections, and addictions and vow complete loyalty to the God of Unapproachable Light (1 Timothy 6:16). It's like we're saying, "God is my God—not porn, alcohol, money, security, popularity, or the approval of others. I worship God and him only."

Worship, therefore, can be a powerful weapon against temptation. A young man recently told me that he was tempted, the previous night, to look at pornography on the Internet. Instead, he pulled away from the computer and sang praise songs to the Lord. Rather than succumbing to sin, he rightfully chose to worship God.

Nothing Better Than God

Worship reinforces the fact that God is infinitely better than anything this world offers. God alone is our lasting satisfaction, our deepest joy, and our greatest pleasure.

Only the Lord can truly satisfy. David told God, "You open your hand; you satisfy the desire of every living thing" (Psalm 145:16). David boasted that the Lord "satisfies you with good so that your youth is renewed like the eagle's" (Psalm 103:5). Psalm 107:9 states that God "satisfies the longing soul, and the hungry soul he fills with good things." John Piper rightly says, "God is most glorified in us when we are most satisfied in him."[27]

Genuine joy—the kind that no one can ever take away—can only be found in the Lord (John 16:22). David discovered a "fullness of joy" in God's presence (Psalm 16:11; 21:6). He sang to God, "You have put more joy in my heart than they have when their grain and wine abound" (Psalm 4:7). Indeed, God is our "exceeding joy" (Psalm 43:4).

Finally, when you think of pleasure, do you think of God?

David exclaimed, "The children of mankind … feast on the abundance of your house, and you give them drink from the river of your delights" (Psalm 36:7–8). "At your right hand are pleasures forevermore" (Psalm 16:11). Notice the rich abundance of all God offers: a "river of delights" and "pleasures forevermore." Why settle for momentary worldly pleasure when we can have the kind of enduring pleasure that God offers, the kind that edifies instead of destroys, liberates instead of enslaves?

The Catholic priest Carlo Carretto poignantly declared that only God can fill the empty void in our hearts:

> To have found God, to have experienced him in the intimacy of our being, to have lived even for one hour in the fire of his Trinity and the bliss of his Unity clearly makes us say: "Now I understand. You alone are enough for me."[28]

May the Holy Spirit grant you the courage to abandon any idols that hinder you from knowing God—and God alone—as your lasting satisfaction, deepest joy, and greatest pleasure.

Ponder and Apply

1 In your opinion, what are the most common examples of modern day idolatry?

2 In what specific ways can obedience be an act of worship for you this week?

3 Can you identify any idols, whether hidden or unhidden, in your life now or in the past? Do your thoughts or actions show any indication that there is something more important to you than God?

4 Following the process outlined in this chapter, how can you go about smashing the idol(s) in your life?

5 Consider the area of your life in which you are most vulnerable to sin and temptation. Write a prayer, like the ones cited in this chapter, invoking the cross and its power over sin.

FOR PASTORS AND WORSHIP LEADERS

If obedience is the highest form of worship, we leaders need to take special care whenever singing or leading songs of commitment. A song like "Have Thine Own Way," for example, should never be taken lightly or sung flippantly. I would suggest that, on occasion, you encourage the congregation to think about the lyrics they're singing to underscore the seriousness of their meaning. Remind them that offering our obedience to Christ is an act of worship.

I have a worship leader friend who put off singing "I Surrender All" for several years because she didn't want to sing anything she didn't mean or wasn't backing up completely with her life. She's a godly woman, but wanted to make sure she was following Christ in every area of her life before she stood up in church and challenged others to do the same. "To say, 'I surrender *all* to Jesus,' is serious business," she told me. "If you're gonna sing it, you better mean it." I couldn't agree more.

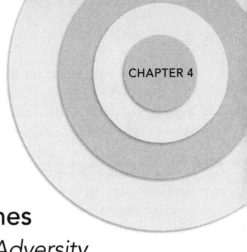

CHAPTER 4

Praise God in the Hard Times
Worship amidst Adversity

It's the most awkward part of a worship leader's job. At least that's how Matt feels every time he stands on the platform waiting to start the service. The congregation is staring at him, expecting him to do something, and all he can do is stand there waiting for the signal to begin.

This morning Matt is very excited about the service. Rehearsals went well and the band sounds tight. Now all he needs is the go-ahead from the sound booth to start. As Matt tunes his guitar, he squints toward the back of the room. Looks like a flurry of activity in the booth. Must be a problem. Matt double-checks his music, trying to look nonchalant. All in order. Still no sign to begin. He glances around the sanctuary. Many are still filtering in, but several hundred are already seated and waiting. Matt checks his E string again. As he looks up, he notices Brian and Kim Wallace walking up the aisle to his left. Matt panics. His mind instantly begins to race and his heart pounds.

Brian and Kim are the nicest couple you'll ever meet. High school sweethearts, they were married at the church seven years ago and have been actively involved in just about every ministry the church offers. For years, Brian and Kim dreamed of starting a family, but struggled to conceive. They consulted every fertility doctor in the area, but still no luck. Everyone in the church was praying for this dear couple.

Then it happened—miracle of miracles! Kim became pregnant! News spread quickly throughout the church. Brian began painting and wallpapering the baby's room. Kim bought maternity clothes. At every baby shower, she recounted with tears of joy how God answered their prayers. "I've never been so happy in all my life," she would say.

About two weeks before her due date, Kim felt painful contractions. The doctor had warned her that the baby could come early. Her water broke and they rushed excitedly to the hospital. After checking in, they got Kim situated in a room and hooked up to a baby monitor. Brian phoned the church and promised to keep everyone updated. Again, word spread throughout the church and, within minutes, people who hardly knew Brian and Kim were praying for them.

As Brian hung up his cell phone, a warning signal suddenly blared from the monitor, and several nurses came running into the room. They worked fast and furiously, all the while bombarding Kim with questions. "When was the last time you felt a contraction?" they asked.

"I don't remember," Kim said.

"Is everything okay?" Brian asked.

The nurses were too busy to reply. Brian began to pray silently.

Their obstetrician arrived and began shouting out orders. More machines. More probing. More questions.

Then an eerie quiet.

The doctor broke the appalling news to Brian and Kim. Somehow, the umbilical cord got wrapped around the baby's neck and cut off circulation. Their baby was dead in the womb. Kim spent the next three hours going through excruciating labor pains, weeping and sweating the whole time, knowing that her baby would be stillborn. It was a boy.

The funeral was held at the church. The sanctuary was packed. The little casket was draped in flowers. Brian and Kim sat in the front row and took turns crying in each other's arms. On a table nearby, the little outfit that their infant son was supposed to wear home from the hospital was stretched out alongside a painting of Jesus holding a child in his arms. Matt attended the service with his parents.

That was two weeks ago. Today is Brian and Kim's first time back at church since the funeral.

The sound engineer tries to get Matt's attention to start the service, but the young worship leader stands frozen, head down, lost in thought. Seeing Brian and Kim raises several unanswered questions for Matt. *Lord, how could you let that happen to such a nice Christian couple? Where were you when they needed you most? Are you or are you not in control?*

Matt finally notices the sound engineer running toward him down the side aisle. "Hey, man, we're ready to start. You okay?"

"Yeah, just give me a minute," Matt replies while fumbling through his music. "I just need to check something." Matt is actually looking over the words to the first couple of songs. When he planned this worship set, he hadn't pictured Brian and Kim sitting in the congregation. *Will any of these songs come off as trite?* he wonders. *Will any of these lyrics sound shallow to Brian and Kim?*

The congregation is growing restless. It's 9:05. Matt bows his head and prays, *Lord, sometimes I feel so inadequate up here. I've never lost a loved one. I'm not even married. I don't know how to lead people like Brian and Kim in worship. Please help me!*

Discussion Questions

1 Why was Matt, the worship leader, overwhelmed when he saw Brian and Kim come into church?

2 What is your reaction to Brian and Kim's story?

3 Why do you think Brian and Kim attended church just two weeks after their baby boy's funeral?

4 Given the situation, do you understand Matt's feelings of inadequacy? Explain.

5 Do you know anybody at your church who is going through hard times? If so, how can you as a church effectively minister to those who are suffering?

Worshiping amidst Adversity

Some of David's psalms have titles indicating the purpose or occasion for which they were written. Psalm 30, for example, was composed for the dedication of the temple. Psalm 51 is a prayer of repentance tied to David's affair with Bathsheba. Many of David's psalms arose from great turmoil.

David faced one difficulty after another and was on the brink of despair on a number of occasions. In other words, David's life experience was much like yours and mine. He was familiar with suffering; he knew all about hardship. In this chapter, we will examine five painful episodes from David's life and the psalms he wrote during those times.

Life this side of heaven is certainly fraught with difficulty. Jesus plainly said, "In the world you will have tribulation" (John

16:33). No one is exempt from pain and suffering. David certainly was no stranger to calamity, and yet he was able to worship amidst adversity.

Down and Discouraged

David was anointed king of Israel at the age of seventeen but wasn't seated on the throne until he was thirty years old. Those intervening years were a time of stormy conflict between David and the incumbent, King Saul. By defeating Goliath and leading the Hebrew army in numerous victories, David won the hearts of the people of Israel. He was so popular, women were singing songs about him: "Saul has struck down his thousands, and David his ten thousands" (1 Samuel 18:7). King Saul didn't like being upstaged by the rookie from rural Bethlehem. Feeling threatened, he set out to kill David. He dispatched hit men to David's house with orders to kill him in the morning. However, in the middle of the night, David's wife, Michal (who coincidentally was Saul's daughter), let David down through a window and he escaped (1 Samuel 19:11 – 17).

Such are the circumstances around which David wrote Psalm 59. He's running for his life; he's discouraged; the outlook is bleak. He begins with an urgent plea for help:

> Deliver me from my enemies, O my God; protect me from those who rise up against me; deliver me from those who work evil, and save me from bloodthirsty men. For behold, they lie in wait for my life; fierce men stir up strife against me.
>
> PSALM 59:1 – 3

Assassins may not be camped outside your door, but you know what it's like to feel defeated and hopeless, like David. Are you feeling down? Are you discouraged in any way? Do you have a difficult person, like Saul, in your life? Someone with whom you have trouble getting along? A coworker, relative, neighbor, or fellow church member who constantly clashes with you?

Though greatly disheartened, David still worshiped, and he was reminded that God is our strength and our fortress: "O my Strength, I will watch for you, for you, O God, are my fortress. My God in his steadfast love will meet me; God will let me look in triumph on my enemies" (Psalm 59:9–10). If you're in the middle of a dicey conflict or the victim of false accusations, may the Lord, "in his steadfast love," meet you, as he did David, and give you strength.

If you're feeling down and discouraged, I suggest you read Psalm 59. And when you get to the last two verses, read them out loud with an air of triumph:

> But I will sing of your strength; I will sing aloud of your steadfast love in the morning. For you have been to me a fortress and a refuge in the day of my distress. O my Strength, I will sing praises to you, for you, O God, are my fortress, the God who shows me steadfast love.
>
> PSALM 59:16–17

Anxious and Afraid

With a contract out on his life, David was a fugitive among his own people. He turned to Achish, the king of Gath, for political asylum. Ironically, Gath was a Philistine stronghold, Goliath's hometown. David was fraternizing with Israel's archenemy. King Achish was sympathetic and granted David sanctuary. However, the king's advisers were suspicious of David's motives. After all, David was the most notorious Philistine killer of all time. "What's he doing here in Gath of all places?" they wondered aloud. "What's David really up to? Is he a traitor or an infiltrator?" Rumors, speculation, and conspiracy theories swirled. Already a marked man in his native Israel, he was certainly no safer in Gath.

Understandably, David was scared to death. The odds were stacked against him. Out of desperation, he pretended to be insane. He started foaming at the mouth and scribbling graffiti on the city walls, like some derelict off the street.

Obviously, this was not David's finest moment. Fear can do strange things to a person. It can lead to irrational thinking and erratic behavior. Fear can be downright paralyzing.

King Achish's response to David's act was rather humorous. "I don't need another nut job in this town," is basically what he said. "I have enough weirdos as it is. Get rid of this guy" (1 Samuel 21:10 – 15). David was once again on the run.

Two of David's psalms were penned during his difficult days in Gath, Psalms 34 and 56. It's no surprise that fear is a major theme woven throughout both psalms.

> Be gracious to me, O God, for man tramples on me; all day long an attacker oppresses me; my enemies trample on me all day long, for many attack me proudly.
>
> PSALM 56:1 – 2

> I sought the LORD, and he answered me and delivered me from all my fears. Oh, fear the LORD you his saints, for those who fear him have no lack!
>
> PSALM 34:4, 9

Are you harboring any doubts or fears these days? Do financial problems, uncertainties at work, or failing health have you on edge? Are you afraid of failure, conflict, or being alone?

David's profound insights about fear are captured eloquently in both psalms. David learned to trust God when afraid (Psalm 56:3 – 4). He learned that God is for us, not against us (Psalm 56:9). With God in the picture, David concluded that he need not fear mere mortals anymore — a healthy fear of God is better than an irrational fear of others (Psalm 34:11 – 22; 56:11). Finally, he remembered that God had delivered him in the past and could always be counted on to intervene again (Psalm 34:4, 6, 19; 56:13).

No wonder David was moved to worship. Though he still had good reason to be afraid, David proclaimed, "My soul makes its boast in the LORD; let the humble hear and be glad. Oh, magnify the LORD with me, and let us exalt his name together!" (Psalm 34:2 – 3).

Frustrated and Disappointed

Saul eventually died and David was crowned king. After settling into the royal palace, David decided to build a house of worship for God's glory. God's response was basically, "Thanks, but no thanks." He told David, "Whereas it was in your heart to build a house for my name, you did well that it was in your heart. Nevertheless, you shall not build the house, but your son who shall be born to you shall build the house for my name" (1 Kings 8:18 – 19). God commended David for the idea, but gave the job instead to David's son Solomon, who eventually erected the renowned Solomon's Temple. David's dream of constructing a temple for God was not only denied but given to someone else.

How about you? Do you have any shattered dreams? Any dashed hopes? Any long-standing unanswered prayers? Are you frustrated by what feels like a dead-end job? Tired of being single? Disappointed with God?

Sometimes God answers our prayers and opens every door along the way. Sometimes God, in his infinite wisdom, denies our requests. Other times, God says, "Wait," because the timing is not right (see Isaiah 64:4).

Then there are times when a dream is from God, but the role he has for us is not what we hoped or imagined. That was certainly the case with David. Instead of a lead role, David would play a supportive, behind-the-scenes role. The temple was his idea, but David wouldn't live long enough to see it started, let alone completed. Nor would he get the credit.

How did David respond? He worshiped. A shattered dream didn't keep David from producing one of the most beautiful expressions of worship ever penned:

> Who am I, O Lord GOD, and what is my house, that you have brought me thus far? Therefore you are great, O LORD God. For there is none like you, and there is no God besides you, according to all that we have heard with our ears.
>
> 2 SAMUEL 7:18, 22

God's denial of David's dream was not the removal of God's blessing. In fact, God turned the tables on David by promising him a privileged role in God's redemptive plan. God envisioned an eternal dynasty for David, one that would establish his throne forever (2 Samuel 7:1 – 17), because the Messiah would come from David's lineage (see Luke 1:32). Again, David responded with grateful worship:

> And your name will be magnified forever, saying, "The LORD of hosts is God over Israel," and the house of your servant David will be established before you. And now, O Lord GOD, you are God, and your words are true, and you have promised this good thing to your servant.
>
> 2 SAMUEL 7:26, 28

In the end, David was at peace with God's decision because he didn't dwell on what he didn't have or what he thought he needed. Instead, he focused on the goodness of God to him.

Devastated and Depressed

Recently, a good friend suggested to me that there is no pain as excruciating as family pain. I couldn't agree more. Family pain can come from without or within; the latter usually cuts deeper, lasts longer, and is far more devastating. Family problems occur between husband and wife, parent and child, or among other family members, and come in various forms: abuse, neglect, anger, bitterness, hatred, broken relationships, dysfunctional behavior, etc. No wonder the term "nuclear family" sounds like a double entendre.

David experienced family strife, most of which centered on his son Absalom. After Absalom's brother Amnon raped their half-sister Tamar, Absalom murdered his brother in retaliation. Absalom then ran away from home and lived estranged from his family for three years. When he returned home to Jerusalem, his father refused to speak to him. So in order to get his dad's attention, Absalom set fire to a nearby field owned by Joab, David's commanding officer. Four years later, Absalom led a coup against his father, and David was once again fleeing for his life. This was one of the lowest points in David's life. Second Samuel 15:30 tells us, "David went up the ascent of the Mount of Olives, weeping as he went, barefoot and with his head covered."

While on the run from Absalom, David wrote Psalm 3, the beginning of which aptly mirrors David's predicament: "O LORD, how many are my foes! Many are rising against me" (Psalm 3:1). Then David recalled how God ministered to him in the past. When he hung his head in shame, God lifted him up (verse 3). He cried to God for help and God answered (verse 4). He slept peacefully in spite of his anxiety because his trust was in the Lord (verse 5).

As is often the case with David, his prayer is laced with worship, and the attributes of God take center stage. He said, "But you, O LORD, are a shield about me" (Psalm 3:3). He goes on to extol God as his sustainer and salvation (Psalm 3:5, 8).

The story of Absalom ends tragically. He was killed in a clash with David's men. When word got back to David, he slipped into a deep depression. Second Samuel 18:33 records David's gut-wrenching lament: "O my son Absalom, my son, my son Absalom! Would I had died instead of you, O Absalom, my son, my son!"

Any parent of a prodigal or a child gone astray can relate to David's anguish. Any mother or father would do anything, trade places if possible, to get a wayward son or daughter back on the straight and narrow. Likewise, many who struggle in a difficult marriage would do anything to have a satisfying relationship with their spouse. Family pain is the heaviest of all burdens.

Weary and Depleted

Psalm 63 was most likely written while David was fleeing from Absalom. Second Samuel 16:14 tells us that "the king, and all the people who were with him, arrived weary at the Jordan." Picture the scene: David's family is torn apart, his kingdom is in crisis, and his reputation severely damaged. He arrives at the Jordan River burned out, beaten down, physically and emotionally exhausted. He bends down at the water's edge and cups his hands to lift some cold clear water to his parched lips. Instead, he buries his face in his hands and cries out, "O God, you are my God; earnestly I seek you; my soul thirsts for you; my flesh faints for you, as in a dry and weary land where there is no water" (Psalm 63:1). What David really needs, and what he desperately cries out for, is a touch from God.

Have you ever felt like that? Hungry for God? Worn out? Emotionally drained? Spiritually dry? Through the prophet Jeremiah, God said, "For I will satisfy the weary soul, and every languishing soul I will replenish" (Jeremiah 31:25). Jesus said, "Come to me, all who labor and are heavy laden, and I will give you rest" (Matthew 11:28).

That's what David did; he sought the Lord. And he came into God's presence worshiping:

> So I have looked upon you in the sanctuary, beholding your power and glory. Because your steadfast love is better than life, my lips will praise you. So I will bless you as long as I live; in your name I will lift up my hands.
>
> PSALM 63:2–4

As David worshiped and meditated on the Lord, he remembered all the times God had come to his aid in the past (Psalm 63:7). As a result, David once again put his hope and trust in God: "My soul clings to you; your right hand upholds me" (Psalm 63:8). David may have been hanging on by a thread, but he was hanging on to God. Psalm 63, which started out as a desperate plea for God, ends with joyous praise at the anticipation of God answering prayer: "But the king shall rejoice in God; all who swear by him shall exult" (Psalm 63:11).

What Happens When We Worship in Tough Times?

Throughout our brief overview of David's life, some obvious themes emerge regarding worship. Let's examine, first of all, the effect that worshiping amid trials has on us.

God Meets Us in Our Time of Need

David learned from firsthand experience that "the Lord is near to the brokenhearted and saves the crushed in spirit" (Psalm 34:18). He discerned that "the LORD is near to all who call on him" (Psalm 145:18). Indeed, God can be found in the midst of our pain and suffering. As David famously wrote, "Even though I walk through the valley of the shadow of death, I will fear no evil, for you are with me" (Psalm 23:4). In fact, in Psalm 18:7 – 19, David describes a God who hastens to come to our rescue: "He rode on a cherub and flew; he came swiftly on the wings of the wind" (Psalm 18:10). David reports that God keeps our tears in a bottle (Psalm 56:8). If you're going through hard times, don't think for a second that God doesn't care. He is fully attentive to your plight. When we seek him during strife and conflict, we receive his comforting, strengthening, life-giving presence.

Our Problems Get Put within God's Larger Context

Left to my own devices, I allow my problems to loom larger than life. Though I may not admit my lack of faith, my worry and anxiety betray the fact that I don't believe God can really handle my dilemma. At that point, my problem is not the real problem. The real crime is that I've made my problem too big and God too small. When I worry, I'm meditating on the presence of my problems, not the presence of God.

That's why David exhorts us to "magnify the LORD" (Psalm 34:3). As we worship, God becomes big again. We are reminded that he is able to do abundantly more than all we could ask or think of asking (Ephesians 3:20). Our problems may not go away, but they are placed firmly within the context of God's sovereignty, power, mercy, and love. Pastor Mark Batterson writes:

> Worship is forgetting about what's wrong with you and remembering what's right with God. It is like hitting the refresh key on your computer. It restores the joy of your salvation. It recalibrates your spirit. It renews your mind. And it enables you to find something good to praise God about even when everything seems to be going wrong.
>
> Is it easy? Absolutely not. Nothing is more difficult than praising God when nothing seems to be going right. But one

of the purest forms of worship is praising God even when you don't feel like it, because it proves that your worship isn't circumstantial.[29]

As Psalm 22 opens, David is facing dire circumstances, and he utters the same words Jesus later cried from the cross: "My God, my God, why have you forsaken me? Why are you so far from saving me, from the words of my groaning? O my God, I cry by day, but you do not answer, and by night, but I find no rest" (Psalm 22:1–2). As David thinks about the Lord, his spirit (as Batterson puts it) is recalibrated. "Yet you are holy, enthroned on the praises of Israel" (Psalm 22:3). Worship reminds us that God is always bigger than any burdens we carry or any challenges we face.

Faith Increases

Psalm 86 opens with David admitting that he is "poor and needy" (Psalm 86:1). "In the day of my trouble I call upon you," he prays (Psalm 86:7). After pleading for help and expressing worship, David then thanks God for answering his prayer: "I give thanks to you, O Lord my God, with my whole heart, and I will glorify your name forever" (Psalm 86:12). Notice that David thanks God before he's delivered. At the end of another lament, David is confident that God will "deal bountifully" with him (Psalm 142:7). When we worship during tough times, faith increases.

Worship bolsters our faith by reminding us that God is good. David wrote, "I believe that I shall look upon the goodness of the LORD in the land of the living!" (Psalm 27:13). David was certain that God is good and that his goodness would always prevail.

Worship also builds our faith by reminding us how the Lord has come to our aid in the past. In Psalm 68:28, David recalls God's faithfulness during previous trials and prays, "Summon your power, O God, the power, O God, by which you have worked for us." Because God had come through for him before, David trusted God during times of duress.

The Bible discloses that Abraham trusted God and "grew strong in his faith as he gave glory to God" (Romans 4:20). Worshiping amidst adversity increases our faith because it reminds us who God is and what he's done in our lives.

We Are Transformed

While worshiping amidst trials, David often expressed a desire to grow in character, to undergo spiritual transformation. In Psalm 25, for example, while feeling "lonely and afflicted" (Psalm 25:16), David prayed, "Make me to know your ways, O LORD; teach me your paths. Lead me in your truth and teach me" (Psalm 25:4–5). In Psalm 86, amidst an impassioned plea for help, David prays, "Teach me your way, O LORD, that I may walk in your truth" (Psalm 86:11). A willingness to be molded and shaped by God was a recurring theme throughout David's private worship, even amid trying times.

God uses trials and tribulations to build our character. Bad things happen, even to good people, because we live in a sinful, broken world. However, God causes all things to work together for good (Romans 8:28). So he is always working to bring good things out of bad circumstances, the most important of which is our spiritual transformation. James 1:2–3 reads, "Count it all joy, my brothers, when you meet trials of various kinds, for you know that the testing of your faith produces steadfastness." By reminding us of God's goodness and grace, worship enables us to remain in the crucible of God's discipline until his transforming work is completed in us.

Furthermore, the apostle Paul wrote, "More than that, we rejoice in our sufferings, knowing that suffering produces endurance, and endurance produces character, and character produces hope" (Romans 5:3–4). Does it sound insensitive to exhort some-one who's hurting to "count it all joy" and "rejoice in suffering"? Exactly how does one do that? Do we put on a happy face and a plastic smile even though our life is in ruins? No, we try, to whatever extent we are honestly able, to offer authentic heartfelt worship.

Peace Abounds

As David worshiped and put his trust in God, he gained a death-defying sense of peace and tranquility. He slept like a baby even when the world around him was falling apart. "In peace I will both lie down and sleep; for you alone, O LORD, make me dwell in safety" (Psalm 4:8). His mourning turned into dancing (Psalm 30:11). His hope was restored (Psalm 39:7). Psalm 94:19 says, "When the cares of my heart are many, your consolations cheer my soul."

When we worship in the bad times, God meets us in our pain and suffering, our problems get put into his larger context, our faith is strengthened, we come through the fiery furnace trans-formed, and that "peace of God, which surpasses all understand-

---

TAKEAWAY #4:
Worship amidst Adversity

Worshiping amidst adversity is easier said than done, but David provides several clues to get us moving in the right direction. Though short, Psalm 54 is a virtual clinic for coping with stress. First, David talks to God about his problems (Psalm 54:1–3). Then David talks to himself about God (verse 4). Finally, David chooses to worship; he offers a sacrifice of praise (verse 6).

ing," settles into our hearts and minds (Philippians 4:7). After all, our God is the "God of all comfort, who comforts us in all our affliction" (2 Corinthians 1:3 – 4).

Speak to God about Your Problem

What do you do when troubles arise? Do you withdraw from God? Give up on church? Stop praying or reading your Bible? Do you overindulge to numb the pain? Overwork to avoid dealing with your issues? Shop or overeat to comfort yourself? Escaping brings only temporary relief and never solves our problems.

David made it a point to run to God, not away from him, during times of crisis. In Psalm 27, he prayed, "Hear, O LORD, when I cry aloud; be gracious to me and answer me! You have said, 'Seek my face.' My heart says to you, 'Your face, LORD, do I seek'" (verses 7 – 8). In the middle of another crisis, David cried out to God, "Be not far from me, for trouble is near, and there is none to help. But you, O LORD, do not be far off! O you my help, come quickly to my aid!" (Psalm 22:11, 19).

Shortly before David became king, ruthless enemies raided the town of Ziklag in Israel and captured the women and children. Having lost their homes and families, David's men were near mutiny. "And David was greatly distressed, for the people spoke of stoning him, because all the people were bitter in soul, each for his sons and daughters. *But David strengthened himself in the LORD his God*" (1 Samuel 30:6, emphasis added). Notice that, for David, God was not a last resort, but the first one he turned to when misfortune set in.

When David spoke to the Lord about his problems, he talked openly and honestly. He knew that God desires "truth in the inward being" (Psalm 51:6). So David never glossed over his sadness. When he was upset, he didn't hide his true feelings.

Be gracious to me, O LORD, for I am in distress; my eye is wasted from grief; my soul and my body also. For my life is spent with sorrow, and my years with sighing.

PSALM 31:9–10

I am weary with my moaning; every night I flood my bed with tears; I drench my couch with my weeping. My eye wastes away because of grief; it grows weak because of all my foes.

PSALM 6:6–7

As you can tell, David poured out his heart to God (Psalm 62:8). He didn't edit his prayers. And he didn't suppress anger, even when he was angry with God. In fact, David often had it out with God: "Why, O LORD, do you stand far away? Why do you hide yourself in times of trouble?" (Psalm 10:1). "How long, O LORD? Will you forget me forever? How long will you hide your face from me?" (Psalm 13:1).

If you find it difficult to come to God when you're hurting, try telling God how you honestly feel. Don't suppress your disappointment, disillusionment, or anger. As David says, "Cast your burden on the LORD, and he will sustain you" (Psalm 55:22).

Speak to Yourself about the Lord

I recently attended a conference that began with a stirring video graphically depicting the pain and suffering that contaminate our world. The woman on the screen kept asking, "Why God? How could you let this happen?" as if the Lord was on trial for committing crimes against humanity. Obviously, the producers of the video wanted viewers to take seriously the oppression and injustice that wreaks havoc in our world. Justice is certainly an important cause that every Christian should take up. However, no mention was made afterward, or any other time during the week, of God's heart for justice and his redeeming work to save mankind.

It's okay to vent your frustration to God. David said, "I pour out my complaint before him; I tell my trouble before him" (Psalm 142:2). If you're disappointed or mad at God, tell him so. But if you stop there, if all you do is rant at God, you will never truly experience God's intimate healing presence.

David not only talked to God about his problems, David spoke to his problems about his God. In Psalm 42:5–6, for example, he said, "Why are you cast down, O my soul, and why are you in turmoil within me? Hope in God; for I shall again praise him, my salvation and my God." David reminds himself of who God is by recalling specific attributes of God. The spotlight shifts from David and his problem and shines on God.

Choose to Worship God Even When Life Is Hard

When the child born from David's affair with Bathsheba fell deathly ill, a distraught David was driven to his knees. For seven days, he fasted and prayed, slept on the ground, and begged the Lord to spare his child's life. When the baby died, David's servants were afraid to tell him for fear that he might harm himself.

> But when David saw that his servants were whispering together, David understood that the child was dead. And David said to his servants, "Is the child dead?" They said, "He is dead." Then David arose from the earth and washed and anointed himself and changed his clothes. And he went into the house of the LORD and worshiped.
>
> 2 SAMUEL 12:19–20

It's easy to praise the Lord when everything is going our way and life is good. It takes an act of will to worship when you don't feel like it—when life is hard. At that point, worship becomes a sacrifice of praise—a dying to self, a concerted effort, and a hard but intentional choice. David proclaimed, "And now my head shall be lifted up above my enemies all around me, and I will offer in his tent sacrifices with shouts of joy; I will sing and make melody to the LORD" (Psalm 27:6). David comes into God's presence with his head down and leaves singing God's praises.

With every trial comes an invitation to worship. God says, "Call upon me in the day of trouble; I will deliver you, and you shall glorify me" (Psalm 50:15). To a first-century church facing persecution, Peter wrote, "So that the tested genuineness of your faith—more precious than gold that perishes though it is tested by fire—may be found to result in praise and glory and honor at the revelation of Jesus Christ" (1 Peter 1:7). God not only allows adversity in order to bring us to maturity but also to see whether we will worship him in the bad times as well as the good. The prophet Habakkuk made a deliberate choice to praise the Lord even when disaster struck:

> Though the fig tree should not blossom, nor fruit be on the vines, the produce of the olive fail and the fields yield no food, the flock be cut off from the fold and there be no herd in the stalls, yet I will rejoice in the LORD; I will take joy in the God of my salvation.
>
> HABAKKUK 3:17–18

No matter what troubles lay ahead, Habakkuk was determined to worship the Lord.

Praising through the Pain

My friend Leo Ahlstrom leads worship at Christ Community Church in St. Charles, Illinois. On June 14, 2009, Leo and his wife, Rebecca, lost their twenty-four-year-old daughter, Meagan, in a tragic automobile accident, the victim of a drunk driver.

Five days later, a service was held at the church to celebrate Meagan's life. The auditorium was packed; friends, family, and church family came out in full force. The service began with a stirring video tribute to Meagan's life. From little girl to young woman, picture after picture revealed a dark-eyed, dark-haired beauty with an infectious smile who obviously loved life, others, and, above all, the Lord. Just days before she died, Meagan quoted Philippians 1:20 in her journal: "I eagerly expect and hope that I will in no way be ashamed, but will have sufficient courage so that now as always Christ will be exalted in my body, whether by life or by death." The next verse goes on to say, "For to me, to live is Christ and to die is gain" (NIV).

After the video montage, Leo got up, welcomed everyone, thanked the church for its support, and read a passage from Psalm 34. Then, with a quivering voice, Leo told his church family, "As a worshiper and a worship pastor, the reason that I wanted to start this service is because I refuse to stand before you on Sunday morning and worship God when things are good and not be willing to worship him when things are not so good."

My friend Leo comes from a long line of worship leaders dating back to David, who somehow found a way to worship God even when life got hard. Without glossing over their pain, they knew that, no matter what happens, God is still sovereign, he is still good, and he is still worthy of our highest praise.

Ponder and Apply

1 What trials, challenges, or hardship are you facing these days?

2 What does it mean to talk to God about your problems?

3 What does it mean to talk to yourself about God when facing difficulty?

4 What have you learned from this chapter that might enable you to worship amidst adversity?

5 What Scriptures minister to you when you're down?

FOR PASTORS AND WORSHIP LEADERS

On any given Sunday, there are people coming to church in desperate need, like Brian and Kim in our opening scenario. Some are facing marital or family problems. Some are unemployed or struggling with problems at work. Others are coping with health issues, suffering chronic pain or illness. Fact is, a lot of folks come to church hurting. They don't need a polished program. They need a genuine encounter with their Creator. We don't have to have all the answers. We just have to be able to point them to the God who does.

As we plan high-impact services, let's keep in mind those in our congregations who are trudging through deep valleys. Let's always avoid trite lyrics in our songs—those that make the Christian life sound like it's a problem-free, pie-in-the-sky cakewalk. Let's be honest about how difficult life is. But let's also preach the Word, pray for each other, and point people to the Lord, in worship.

PART 2

Growing as a Corporate Worshiper

Worship in the Book of Revelation

An elderly woman at church stopped me between services not long ago, eager to share exciting news. She had attended a "hymn sing" at a neighboring church and couldn't wait to tell me about it. She brought me a copy of the program, which looked to contain about two hours' worth of music. "We sang all my old favorites," she exclaimed, "the great hymns of the faith. I thought I had died and gone to heaven."

Now I'm fond of hymns, but her comment made me wonder what worship in heaven is really like. Certainly heaven is going to be more than just an eternal hymn sing, more than just choir and pipe organ or, for that matter, drums and guitar all the time. No matter how fantastic the worship is at your church,

I wouldn't assume that it always accurately represents heaven. So what does worship in heaven look like? What does it sound like? And what can we learn from heavenly worship that can help us become better worshipers now?

Worship in Heaven

In the first section of this book, we discussed the spiritual discipline of private worship. David served as our example and guide. Private fellowship with the Lord is wonderful but there is an exciting dimension to worship that can only be experienced in the company of other believers. In the remaining chapters, we will look at the book of Revelation, with its jaw-dropping description of heavenly worship, and learn how to become better corporate worshipers. We will examine worship as it is in heaven and glean insights we can apply here on earth right now. So think of the second half of this book as an instruction manual for churchgoers, a guide on how to worship more meaningfully every Sunday at church.

By the way, we won't leave David behind, for he was an avid public worshiper. "In the midst of the congregation I will praise you," he wrote in Psalm 22:22. "I will praise him in the midst of the throng" (Psalm 109:30). David loved being in God's house, worshiping with God's people. "O LORD, I love the habitation of your house," he declared, "and the place where your glory dwells" (Psalm 26:8). And in Psalm 122:1, he exclaimed, "I was glad when they said to me, 'Let us go to the house of the LORD!'" It just goes to show that private worshipers make the best corporate worshipers.

The Tabernacle

There is precedence for looking heavenward for instruction

concerning worship. Ancient Israel patterned its worship after heaven's model. As you recall, the Jews, after being freed from exile in Egypt, wandered in the desert for forty years. Early on, they realized they needed a gathering place for worship. God directed them to build a huge portable tent called the tabernacle. In Exodus 25–28, God gave detailed instructions on what the tabernacle and the other sacred symbols of worship should look like and how they were to be created. Hebrews 8:5 reports that the tabernacle was a "copy and shadow of the heavenly things" (see also Hebrews 9:23). This mobile sanctuary was patterned after heavenly realities.

The Number One Activity

As previously stated in chapter 1, worship is the primary activity in heaven: "No longer will there be anything accursed, but the throne of God and of the Lamb will be in it, and his servants will worship him" (Revelation 22:3). John MacArthur writes: "In Revelation we learn that all of history culminates in an eternal worshiping community in the presence of a loving God."[30] Psalm 115:18 states that "we will bless the LORD from this time forth and forevermore." A. W. Tozer argues that if you don't like worship, you're not going to enjoy heaven:

> I can safely say, on the authority of all that is revealed in the Word of God, that any man or woman on this earth who is bored and turned off by worship is not ready for heaven.[31]

Are We Really Ready for Heavenly Worship?

Tozer poses an interesting question: Are you ready for heaven and all the worship we'll experience there? Lest you think you need no preparation or orientation for heavenly worship, I must warn you that worship in heaven is unlike anything you've ever experienced. It's like worship on steroids. You may be surprised to discover that various aspects of heavenly worship are unfamiliar to your experience; they may even seem completely foreign to you.

It's Loud!

First of all, heavenly worship is scandalously loud:

> Then I looked, and I heard around the throne and the living creatures and the elders the voice of many angels, numbering myriads of myriads and thousands of thousands, saying with a loud voice ...
>
> REVELATION 5:11–12

> Then the seventh angel blew his trumpet, and there were loud voices in heaven, saying ...
>
> REVELATION 11:15

> After this I heard what seemed to be the loud voice of a great multitude in heaven, crying out ...
>
> REVELATION 19:1

John hears "the voice of a great multitude, like the roar of many waters and like the sound of mighty peals of thunder" (Revelation 19:6; see also Revelation 7:10 and 14:2). He describes "flashes of lightning, rumblings, peals of thunder, an earthquake, and heavy hail" (Revelation 11:19). Indeed, heaven is not a quiet place.

I'm a big fan of contemplative worship, and I believe heaven will include plenty of opportunities for quiet reflection. After all, Revelation chapter 8 opens with silence and prayer. However, when heaven worships, the volume generally goes way up. For some of us, that may take some getting used to.

Every church that features contemporary music faces controversy over volume levels. Such churches field complaints that the music is too loud. I encourage compassion toward anyone who may be sensitive to loud sounds, but some people take their complaining way too far. They're rude to the ushers and the sound team. They stomp out of church angry and write nasty letters. Recently I saw a disgruntled man and his wife create an ugly scene at church by standing with their fingers planted firmly in their ears, scowls on their faces, during the entire worship set. I can't help but wonder how those folks will fare amidst the deafeningly loud sounds of thunder, earthquakes, and trumpets that await them in heaven's worship.

One woman pointed out to me recently that our heavenly bodies will be better and stronger, much more tolerant to loud noise. First Corinthians 15:40–44 does say that our heavenly bodies will be glorious and imperishable. But who's to say whether that'll make our hearing more tolerant or more sensitive? John was a frail old man when he caught a glimpse of heaven, and when he mentions how loud it is, he doesn't sound at all like he's complaining about it.

Furthermore, the Bible contains many examples of loud worship this side of heaven. In 2 Chronicles 20:19, we are told that Israel's worship leaders "stood up to praise the LORD, the God of Israel, with a very loud voice." During Jesus' triumphant entry into Jerusalem "the whole multitude of his disciples began to rejoice and praise God with a loud voice for all the mighty works that they had seen" (Luke 19:37). Therefore, loud celebratory praise has a rightful place in worship.

It's Repetitive

People may also be surprised to learn that heavenly worship is sometimes repetitive. Revelation 4:8 reveals this fascinating tidbit concerning the four living creatures around God's throne: "*Day and night they never cease* to say, 'Holy, holy, holy, is the Lord God Almighty, who was and is and is to come!'" (emphasis added). Because these four creatures live every minute in God's immediate presence, they never grow tired or bored of repeating the same thing over and over: "Holy, holy, holy, is the Lord God Almighty, who was and is and is to come!" A similar description can be found in Isaiah 6:1–3, written several hundred years earlier, thus confirming the fact that this worshipful scene occurs over and over again in heaven.

Unfortunately, some people get annoyed when asked to sing the same chorus again and again. And again! I heard of one pastor who got so fed up with his worship leader repeating a certain line of a song that he impatiently yelled out, "Okay, we got it already. Let's move on." That pastor may speak for those who share his frustration, but if heaven is any indication, repetition has its rightful place during worship. Apparently, words that adamantly extol God are worth repeating.

Be Teachable

In light of what worship in heaven is really like, some of our preconceived notions about corporate worship may need to be reevaluated. You might not have an issue with music volume or repetition, but you might take exception to a certain style of worship. Perhaps you're offended by a particular kind of music. Sadly, in too many churches today, battle lines are drawn along musical styles—traditional vs. contemporary, contemporary vs. even more contemporary, etc. I know a woman whose father is no longer speaking to her because she's spearheading the contemporary service at her church. As an elder at the church, her father is vehemently opposed to current worship styles. God intended corporate worship to be a beautiful expression of Christian unity. It must break God's heart when we allow worship to become a source of strife and division.

To grow as corporate worshipers, one must first be teachable. Ecclesiastes 5:1 suggests we always come to church ready to listen and learn: "Guard your steps when you go to the house of God. To draw near to listen is better than to offer the sacrifice of fools, for they do not know that they are doing evil." So be open-minded, especially when it comes to worship.

When King David introduced new instruments into corporate worship (1 Chronicles 23:5), the Bible makes no mention of anyone complaining about these newfangled innovations. Or if anyone did object, the writers of Scripture didn't think it was worth mentioning. In the same way, let's not be too quick to dismiss worship styles, old or new, that are different from what we're used to. Instead of judging a different approach by whether you like it or not, evaluate it on the basis of whether or not it contradicts Scripture. If a certain practice does nothing for you, respect and appreciate the possibility that it may enhance worship for others.

Start Preparing for Heavenly Worship Now

In the ensuing chapters, we will explore four compelling features of heavenly worship. We'll discover that worship in heaven is all four:

- pure ascription
- unapologetically passionate
- intergenerational
- multiethnic

Each of those characteristics has implications for believers whenever we gather to worship. It doesn't matter whether your church is big or small, traditional or contemporary, denominational or not, the principles we'll learn apply to all settings.

Jesus is preparing a place for us in heaven. He said, "In my Father's house are many rooms. If it were not so, would I have told you that I go to prepare a place for you? And if I go and prepare a place for you, I will come again and will take you to myself, that where I am you may be also" (John 14:2–3). Commenting on this passage, author Randy Alcorn wisely wrote, "Christ is not simply preparing a place for us; he is preparing us for that place."[32] Part of our preparation for heaven involves us growing as worshipers.

Therefore, every church service here on earth is preparation for the real thing—a rehearsal for the glorious praise gatherings we'll experience in paradise. So next Sunday morning as you head out the door, remember that you're not just going to church, you're going to worship practice.

CHAPTER 5

You Are Worthy, O Lord!
Focus on God's Attributes

Sean and Megan slide into the last pew in the back, extremely exhausted. They smile and greet those around them warmly, but no one else has any idea how much effort it took for them to get to church this morning. Getting their three kids out of bed, dressed, fed, and packed into the car is a prodigious feat on any day, but this morning's drill was compounded by several mishaps. First, their oldest son, Ricky, emptied an entire box of cereal onto the kitchen floor. As the grown-ups were cleaning up and restoring order, Lisa, the middle child, decided to explore her mom's makeup kit. During the chaos that ensued, the dog forgot two years of house training and conducted business on the hallway carpet. Then the baby spit up all over Megan as they were heading out the door, so Mom had to run in and quickly change clothes. All in all, it's a small miracle that Sean and Megan are even in church this morning. However, it remains to be seen just how "there" they really are.

As the first worship song begins, everyone stands. Sean and Megan enthusiastically join in. However, midway through the second verse, Sean starts thinking about work. He is under a lot of pressure at the office these days and has a lot on his plate. While still mouthing the words to the song, Sean rehearses in his mind a presentation he's scheduled to give tomorrow for his boss.

Meanwhile, Megan sings and claps as the worship team launches into an upbeat version of the old hymn "All Hail the Power of Jesus' Name." But soon her mind begins to wander. There's a soccer game after church, and Megan now remembers it's their turn to bring half-time treats. The back of the bulletin becomes a makeshift grocery list. Then her mind starts racing through all sorts of soccer-related issues: *Why are soccer games always played on Sundays? Why are the uniforms so expensive? And why doesn't the coach play Ricky more often? It's not fair. He never misses practice; always tries his hardest. I'm afraid this coach has his favorites and leaves out the other kids. I think I should talk to him after the game today. Why ...*

The song ends, and everyone sits down as a pleasant young man steps up to the front to give the announcements. Sean immediately tunes out. His thoughts go to a coworker with whom he has problems getting along. *This guy has been against me since day one,* Sean thinks. *He's been a thorn in my side for years. I try to be nice, but he stabs me in the back. What have I ever done to him? He's so negative; it drives me crazy! It might be time to start looking for another job. I wish I had gone into professional sports. Now there's a dream job ...*

Sean quietly slips into his favorite sports fantasy. He's playing tight end for the Dallas Cowboys. It's the Super Bowl. Cowboys are losing, 28–24. Fourth quarter. The ball is on the opponent's ten-yard line. One second left on the clock. Last play of the game. The ball is snapped, Sean runs a perfect post pattern, splits the seams in the defense. The pass is wide. Sean reaches out and brings it in with one hand and then dives into the end zone. The fans go crazy! Cameras flashing! Sean triumphantly spikes the ball into the ground. His teammates hoist him on their shoulders and carry him off the field ...

After the offering, the worship leader reads a Scripture passage and invites everyone to pray and worship silently for a couple minutes. Megan can't help but notice that one of the women on the worship team is wearing her hair differently. *She looks good with her hair that way, Megan thinks. It's time I got a different hairstyle. I wonder if I should cut my hair. I definitely need to start coloring it. I sure wish I could find a hairdresser I trust ...*

Megan catches herself daydreaming and closes her eyes to pray. It's quiet in the sanctuary, the first peaceful moment she's had in months. *Lord,* she prays, *I'm sorry my mind keeps drifting. Life is pretty hectic these days and I'm always so tired. Help me to hear your voice and feel your presence.* She pauses, not knowing what to say next. She slowly opens one eye to check on Sean ... he's fast asleep.

Discussion Questions

1 Why do both Sean and Megan find it difficult to concentrate during church?

2 How common is it for people to become distracted during worship?

3 What factors might contribute to one's inability to stay focused throughout a worship service?

4 Do you see any irony in Sean entertaining a self-glorifying sports fantasy at a time when he's supposed to be glorifying God? If so, explain.

5 Do you ever get distracted during worship? If so, what do you do to stay engaged?

Pure Ascription

At this very moment, all heaven is breaking loose in glorious worship. The heavenly throng is exclaiming:

> Holy, holy, holy, is the Lord God Almighty, who was and is and is to come!
>
> REVELATION 4:8

> Worthy are you, our Lord and God, to receive glory and honor and power, for you created all things, and by your will they existed and were created.
>
> REVELATION 4:11

Heaven's worship is not focused on us but solely on God. The result is pure ascription—worship that is obsessed with God's intrinsic worth and ascribes to God alone the glory and honor due him. There are no personal pronouns recorded in heaven's worship—no "me," no "my," no "I." Instead, the names and attributes of God are front and center: "Blessing and glory and wisdom and thanksgiving and honor and power and might be to our God forever and ever! Amen" (Revelation 7:12). Everyone in heaven is so enamored with God that they don't waste a single moment thinking only about themselves.

Ascriptive worship reminds us that we are not the center of the universe; God is. He is set apart, distinct from us. He is the Creator; we are the created. He is infinite; we are finite. He is holy and righteous; we are broken and sin-prone. Thus, ascriptive worship resizes us, putting us in proper relationship to God. "Praise our God, all you his servants, you who fear him, small and great" (Revelation 19:5).

In heaven, just like on earth, God is worshiped not only for who he is but also for what he's done: "Great and amazing are your deeds, O Lord God the Almighty! Just and true are your ways.... All nations will come and worship you, for your righteous acts have been revealed" (Revelation 15:3–4).

The atoning work of God in Christ, the pinnacle of God's wondrous deeds, is the subject of much of heaven's worship. We will bow before the Lamb of God and sing:

> "Worthy are you to take the scroll and to open its seals, for you were slain, and by your blood you ransomed people for God.... Worthy is the Lamb who was slain, to receive power and wealth and wisdom and might and honor and glory and blessing!... To him who sits on the throne and to the Lamb be blessing and honor and glory and might forever and ever!"
>
> REVELATION 5:9, 12–13

Heavenly worship overflows with thanksgiving. Worshiping God for who he is and what he's done ignites an overwhelming sense of gratitude. Those gathered in God's presence "give glory and honor and thanks to him who is seated on the throne" (Revelation 4:9). The twenty-four elders fall before God and say, "We give thanks to you, Lord God Almighty, who is and who was, for you have taken your great power and begun to reign" (Revelation 11:17). Revelation 7:12 proclaims, "Blessing and glory and wisdom and thanksgiving ... be to our God." Praise and thanksgiving go hand in hand; they are the lifeblood of Christian worship, a natural response to God, for all he's done and continues to do.

The Otherness of God

Ascriptive worship acknowledges that God is not like us; he is in a class by himself, and it's the highest, greatest, and loftiest class of all. He is totally and Absolutely Other. Matt Redman describes the "otherness" of God as

> a sense that God is so pure, matchless and unique that no one

else and nothing else even comes close. He is altogether glorious—unequalled in splendor and unrivalled in power. He is beyond the grasp of human reason—far above the reach of even the loftiest scientific mind. Inexhaustible, immeasurable and unfathomable—eternal, immortal and invisible. The highest mountain peaks and the deepest canyon depths are just tiny echoes of His proclaimed greatness. And the blazing stars above, the faintest emblems of the full measure of His glory.[33]

Expressions of pure ascription, therefore, reflect this "otherness" of God and compel us to approach the Lord in reverence. In Hebrews 12, we are instructed to "offer to God acceptable worship, with reverence and awe, for our God is a consuming fire" (verses 28–29). In Psalm 96:9, we are told, "Worship the LORD in the splendor of holiness; *tremble* before him, all the earth!" (emphasis added). Worshipers are to come before God in complete submission and humility.

A good example is the hymn "Holy, Holy, Holy."[34] In the span of four stanzas, God is referred to as "Lord God Almighty," "God in three Persons," and "blessed Trinity." He is presented as holy, merciful, mighty, eternal, incomparable, and perfect in power, love, and purity. Furthermore, there is no mention of us as individuals. Instead, the names and attributes of God are highlighted first and foremost. No wonder this classic hymn is a favorite of worshipers all over the world.

Heaven's Antidote
for Our Narcissism and Discontent

In their book *The Narcissism Epidemic: Living in the Age of Entitlement*, authors Jean M. Twenge and Keith Campbell provide alarming evidence that our culture is becoming increasingly narcissistic. Studying data from a test known as the Narcissistic Personality Inventory, the authors found a 30 percent increase in narcissistic tendencies among college students over the last two decades. Recently, one out of four college students taking the same test gave answers leaning toward narcissism.[35] In the book's introduction, the authors provide plenty of illustrations:

> On a reality TV show, a girl planning her sixteenth birthday party wants a major road blocked off so a marching band can precede her grand entrance on a red carpet.... It is now possible to hire fake paparazzi to follow you around snapping your photograph when you go out at night — you can even take home a faux celebrity magazine cover featuring the pictures. A popular song declares, with no apparent sarcasm, "I believe that the world should revolve around me!" ... Babies wear bibs embroidered with "Supermodel" or "Chick Magnet" and suck on "Bling" pacifiers while their parents read modernized nursery rhymes from *This Little Piggy Went to Prada.*... High school students pummel classmates and then seek attention for their violence by posting YouTube videos of the beatings.[36]

Before condemning such self-absorbed behavior, we'd better be ready to confront any and all selfishness in our own hearts. Human beings are notoriously self-centered, always looking out for Number One. All too often, we put our emotional needs ahead of the needs of others, sometimes at the expense of others. Our bottom line for everything — whether it be work, relationships, marriage, or even church — is too often, "What's in it for me?"

Our narcissistic tendencies are as problematic on Sunday mornings as any other morning. I can sing praise songs at the top of my lungs with hands in the air with all my thoughts centered on me. I can sing while daydreaming about scoring the winning touchdown in the Super Bowl. When the words coming from my lips are contradicted by what's happening in my mind and heart, I have failed to worship God. D. A. Carson reasons that "we cannot ascribe to the Lord all the glory due his name if we are consumed by self-love or intoxicated by pitiful visions of our own greatness or independence."[37]

It's Not about You

Worship that is pure ascription—focused not on us, but solely on God—gets our eyes off ourselves and onto the Lord. It is a biblical way to worship! Psalm 115:1 says, "Not to us, O LORD, not to us, but to your name give glory." Worship is not about us, as though it is an opportunity for us to show how zealous and spiritual we are. It's entirely about the Lord. Like John the Baptist, we must come to each worship service with a mindset that says, "He must increase, but I must decrease" (John 3:30).

In Ezekiel 44:16, God instructs the priests to "enter my sanctuary ... to minister to me." Worship, therefore, is something we offer God. It's not a show the church puts on to make us feel good or to motivate us. Worship is something we do to honor God.

Unholy Discontent

Narcissism inevitably leads to discontent, because living solely for oneself never brings true happiness. Henry David Thoreau said, "The mass of men lead lives of quiet desperation." With all due respect, most of us are not all that quiet about our unhappiness. Whether you're listening to coworkers around the water cooler, your kids in the minivan, or talk radio during the afternoon commute, it seems to be human nature to grumble and complain, though most of us are blessed with far more than we deserve.

Our heavenly Father doesn't care for complaining; it offends him. Note his reaction to the people of Israel: "And the people complained in the hearing of the LORD about their misfortunes, and when the LORD heard it, his anger was kindled" (Numbers 11:1). Complaining is an insult to God. It's like saying, "God, I don't trust that you're good. I think you're holding out on me, and I can't be happy unless you give me what I want." Truth is, God has never let us down and he never will. "And from his fullness we have all received, grace upon grace" (John 1:16).

Be a Worshiper, Not a Complainer

While complaining offends God, gratitude pleases him. Jesus told a story about ten lepers who were healed, lamenting the fact that only one, a Samaritan, returned to give thanks. Jesus asked, "Were not ten cleansed? Where are the nine? Was no one found to return and give praise to God except this foreigner?" (Luke 17:17 – 18). I imagine the disciples thinking, *Note to self: When God blesses, don't forget to thank him.* If I were to get a tattoo (which would be totally out of character, but fun to think about), I'd have that same line inscribed on my arm as a constant reminder of how important gratitude is to God.

It's uncanny how often the Bible reminds us to "give thanks." In fact, that friendly reminder is tacked on to just about anything and everything we do:

- Preparing for battle? Give thanks (2 Chronicles 20:21).
- Is it the Sabbath? Give thanks (Psalm 92:1).
- On your way to church? Give thanks (Psalm 100:4).
- Presenting an offering? Give thanks (Psalm 107:22).
- Sitting down to eat? Give thanks (1 Timothy 4:3).

- Thinking about telling a dirty joke? Give thanks instead (Ephesians 5:4).

- Feeling anxious? Give thanks (Philippians 4:6).

- Want to model spiritual maturity? Abound in thanksgiving (Colossians 2:7).

- Want true peace? Give thanks (Colossians 3:15).

- Praying? Give thanks (Colossians 4:2).

First Thessalonians 5:18 sums it up nicely: "Give thanks in all circumstances; for this is the will of God in Christ Jesus for you."

Why does the Bible keep nagging us to give thanks? It's because we quickly forget all that God has done for us; we take him for granted. According to Romans 1:21, when we fail to honor God and give him thanks, our hearts become darkened. Indeed, if left unchecked, ingratitude leads to negativity, bitterness, cynicism, and despair.

Though discontent runs rampant in our modern age, followers of Christ are called to be worshipers, not complainers. Pastor Mark Batterson says,

> There are basically two types of people in the world: complainers and worshipers. And there isn't much circumstantial difference between the two. Complainers will always find something to complain about. Worshipers will always find something to praise God about. They simply have different default settings.[38]

Thanksgiving is the antidote for discontentment, keeping it from taking root in our hearts. Many of the corporate gatherings described in Scripture include giving thanks. When the Israelites brought the ark of the covenant to Jerusalem, the theme of their celebration was gratitude (1 Chronicles 16:7 – 34). There was even a group of men involved who were "chosen and expressly named to give thanks to the LORD" (1 Chronicles 16:41). Offering thanks was their job description. Their business cards read: "Minister of Thanksgiving." The original purpose behind using musical instruments in worship was to give thanks (2 Chronicles 7:6; see also Psalm 33:2). Under Nehemiah's leadership, there was a group of men who were "in charge of the songs of thanksgiving" (Nehemiah 12:8); they even had two thanksgiving choirs (Nehemiah 12:31, 38, 40). Imagine a choir dedicated exclusively to singing songs of thanksgiving!

Church, therefore, is a place where worship and thanksgiving go hand in hand—a place to sing "psalms and hymns and spiritual songs, with thankfulness in your hearts to God" (Colossians 3:16). In Psalm 111:1, David underscores the value of expressing thanks to God in church: "I will give thanks to the LORD with my whole heart, in the company of the upright, in the congregation." Psalm 35:18 adds, "I will thank you in the great congregation; in the mighty throng I will praise you." Serious worshipers, therefore, come to church ready to offer praise and thanksgiving to our gracious God.

It Is Enough

During the Jewish feast of Passover, there is a song that is sung or recited that expresses gratitude in a unique way. The song is called the "Dayenu" (pronounced DIE-yea-noo), a Hebrew word meaning "it would have been enough for us" or "it would have sufficed." That phrase is repeated in response to a long list of God's blessings on behalf of the people of Israel. Here's a brief sampling:

- Had God brought us out of Egypt but not executed judgments against the Egyptians, *it would have been enough for us.*

- Had God given us their wealth but not split the sea for us, *it would have been enough for us.*
- Had God split the sea for us but not let us through it on dry land, *it would have been enough for us.*
- Had God provided for our needs in the desert for forty years but not fed us the manna, *it would have been enough for us.*

The point is that it would have been enough had God done just one of those things. Yet God didn't stop there, but kept adding, and continues to add, blessing upon blessing. If you're ever discontented or you find yourself slipping into a what-have-you-done-for-me-lately attitude toward God, consider all he's done and continues to do in your life. "Remember the wondrous works that he has done, his miracles, and the judgments he uttered" (Psalm 105:5). If the only blessing we ever received was salvation through Jesus Christ, that would certainly be enough. But God has given us so much more. "I will give thanks to the LORD with my whole heart; I will recount all of your wonderful deeds" (Psalm 9:1).

TAKEAWAY #5:

Focus on God's Attributes during Corporate Worship

The names and attributes of God played a major role in the discipline of private worship, and they loom large as we practice corporate worship. If you want to worship on earth as they do in heaven, if you want to offer praise that is pure ascription, focus on God's majestic attributes and marvelous deeds when you gather for worship.

Worship God for Who He Is

"Ascribe to the LORD, O heavenly beings, ascribe to the LORD glory and strength," writes David. "Ascribe to the LORD the glory due his name; worship the LORD in the splendor of holiness" (Psalm 29:1 – 2). One practical way to ascribe to God the honor he deserves is to be on the lookout for names and attributes of God during corporate worship, especially in hymns and praise choruses. Whether the lyrics are sung from a hymnbook, printed in the bulletin, or flashed on a screen, pay special attention to any names or attributes of God that you feel especially drawn to. Sing those words louder or with greater emphasis. You could even say a quiet (or loud) "Amen" at that point. Or you could choose not to sing, but bow your head in quiet reverence. You may even ask the Lord to reveal more of that name or attribute to you. In Psalm 68:34 – 35, David exclaims, "Ascribe power to God, whose majesty is over Israel, and whose power is in the skies. Awesome is God from his sanctuary; the God of Israel — he is the one who gives power and strength to his people. Blessed be God!" Focusing on the names and attributes of God inevitably compels us to worship him.

Minimizes Distractions

Does your mind ever wander when you're at church? Mine sure does. Over the years, there have been numerous times when Sue and I have been driving home from church, and she'll start elaborating on one of the points of the sermon or a line from a song that ministered to her. Her perplexed husband looks back at her as if to say, "What insight? What sermon? What song?" It all went completely over my head. Much like Sean and Megan in our opening scenario, my thoughts sometimes scatter, flitting from one thing to another, as I sit through the service. My mouth may be moving, but my mind is elsewhere. I'm often convicted by Jesus' words in Matthew 15:8 – 9: "This people honors me with their lips, but their heart is far from me; in vain do they worship me." If you too have difficulty being fully present during church, try going on the alert for names and attributes of God, especially in the lyrics of praise songs and hymns. I have found that focusing on God's character helps me stay engaged and brings me back when my mind wanders.

Gives a Greater Sense of God's Presence

As we observed with private worship, honing in on the names or attributes of God offers a greater sense of God's presence during corporate gatherings as well. R. C. Sproul points out:

> A Christian service of worship is a gathering of God's people in His presence; it is an encounter with God. So how can we account for the results of the polls that tell us that people come away from church feeling that it is boring and irrelevant?
>
> I believe it is because they have no sense of the presence of God when they attend worship. The real crisis of worship today is not that the preaching is paltry or that it's too drafty in church. It is that people have no sense of the presence of God, and if they have no sense of His presence, how can they be moved to express the deepest feelings of their souls to honor, revere, worship, and glorify God?[39]

Zooming in on the attributes of God leaves a lasting impression of God's presence and prevents worship from ever becoming boring or irrelevant.

Curbs Negativity

I've been involved in church work all my life, and I love the local church. I also love worshiping with fellow believers. However,

I've discovered that church folk can also be some of the most negative people you'll ever meet. They complain about the most trivial things. At one church where I worked, a man sent the pastor a note complaining that the cookie he received at the welcome booth on Sunday morning was "too soggy." Another groused that our worship leader said "exult" instead of "exalt." (I honestly couldn't hear the difference.)

Nothing draws more complaints from churchgoers than the music. Music is highly subjective; people have strong feelings about what they like and dislike. So you're bound to hear some songs in church you don't like and might even hate. You may also be subjected to music that is played or sung poorly. I once heard a worship band go through an entire song playing in two different keys—and no one on the platform even appeared to notice. Most church musicians are good-hearted amateurs. They mean well, but that doesn't mean they always play well. That's why it's important to concentrate on the message, not the messengers. If you're tuned in to the attributes of God, you will be able to worship regardless of the style or quality of the music.

Several years ago I was invited to speak at a conference in Indianapolis. When I walked into the arena and noticed that the majority of the conference attendees were older and grayer than I am, I felt a little out of place. But when the worship started, I was right at home. The music was not my cup of tea, but the lyrics were Christ-centered. A couple attributes of God jumped out at me and inspired me to praise the Lord. A few days later, I attended a worship service for twentysomethings. The music was very loud, and there was a lot of youthful jumping around on stage. But I knew the leaders. They love Jesus. The words up on the screen were just as worshipful as any I had ever heard. And again, I had a wonderful time worshiping the Lord. Two different worship experiences, two completely diverse styles of music, but I was able to worship because I allowed the attributes of God to transcend my musical preferences and shape my worship. Hopefully what drives you on Sunday mornings is not how much you love the music, but how much you love the Lord.

Thank God for All He's Done

Look for opportunities to express gratitude throughout the service. The prophet Samuel reminds us to "consider what great things he has done for you" (1 Samuel 12:24). "Gratitude," writes Thomas Merton, "takes nothing for granted, is never unresponsive, is constantly awakening to new wonder and to praise of the goodness of God. For the grateful man knows that God is good, not by hearsay but by experience."[40] Giving thanks is not something anyone else can do for you. So during church, as the Spirit prompts, be sure to thank God for all he's done and continues to do throughout the world and in your life.

For example, anytime salvation or the cross is mentioned, whether in a song, prayer, or Bible reading, thank Jesus for laying down his life for you. Paul wrote, "The saying is trustworthy and deserving of full acceptance, that Christ Jesus came into the world to save sinners, of whom I am the foremost.... To the King of ages, immortal, invisible, the only God, be honor and glory forever and ever. Amen" (1 Timothy 1:15, 17). As Paul clearly demonstrates, meditating on the cross leads naturally to heartfelt gratitude and passionate worship.

Communion is another obvious opportunity to express gratitude. Even Christ, when he instituted this sacred sacrament, did so with a thankful heart.

The Lord Jesus on the night when he was betrayed took bread,

and when he had given thanks, he broke it, and said, "This is
my body which is for you. Do this in remembrance of me."
1 CORINTHIANS 11:23–24, EMPHASIS ADDED

Furthermore, in the original Greek and Latin, the word *Eucharist* means "giving thanks," reminding us to take the bread and
the cup with deep gratitude for the ultimate sacrifice Christ made
for us.

There are other parts of a typical church service that provide
opportunities to give thanks, like the offering. Psalm 96:8 confirms that giving an offering is an act of worship: "Ascribe to the
LORD the glory due his name; bring an offering, and come into
his courts!" Indeed, the offering is another golden opportunity to
tell God, "Thank you!" Paul stated, "You will be enriched in every
way to be generous in every way, which through us will produce
thanksgiving to God" (2 Corinthians 9:11). As you drop your tithe
in the offering plate, thank God for his continued blessings and
provision in your life. Make the offering a worshipful experience.

If someone shares a testimony or is baptized, why not quietly thank God for saving yet another lost soul? David exclaimed,
"May those who love your salvation say evermore, 'God is great!'"
(Psalm 70:4). Also, be sure to thank God for your own conversion
and all that the Lord has done in your life since. Again, David
implores us to "tell of his salvation" (Psalm 96:2) and "tell what
God has brought about and ponder what he has done" (Psalm
64:9).

Let Jesus Be Your Worship Leader

Being proactive during church is the way you engage in meaningful worship. Don't punch out during worship. Don't daydream,
oblivious to God's presence. And don't wait for the pastor or

worship leader to point out attributes of God or prompt you to give thanks. The worship team may kick off the service, the choir might sing a "call to worship," but God is the one who truly initiates worship. Every worship experience recorded in the Bible begins with God revealing himself to undeserving human beings who then respond with praise and adoration. As you sit in church, let the Lord reveal himself to you. "Draw near to God, and he will draw near to you" (James 4:8).

Remember that Jesus is not only present wherever two or three have gathered together in his name (Matthew 18:20), he also participates in worship. In fact, he is The Worship Leader of all worship leaders, always pointing people to the Father (John 12:28; 17:1, 4) "in order that in everything God may be glorified through Jesus Christ" (1 Peter 4:11). Furthermore, Hebrews 2:12 reveals that Christ joins in our worship. Jesus says, "I will tell of your name to my brothers; in the midst of the congregation I will sing your praise." Imagine that! Jesus sings along during our worship! Therefore, look to him as your worship leader.

The Holy Spirit also plays an active role during worship. The Spirit glorifies Christ (John 16:14). Philippians 3:3 points out that we worship "by the Spirit of God and glory in Christ Jesus." Notice the presence of the Trinity during worship. We worship the Father, through the Son, in the Spirit. The Trinity, therefore, is a worshiping community—one into which we are invited every time we heed the call to worship. So as you walk into church, think of yourself as an active participant, not a casual observer, in the fellowship of the Trinity. In short, think of yourself as a vibrant worshiper.

In conclusion, let's eagerly praise the Lord for who he is and what he's done: "For you are great and do wondrous things; you alone are God" (Psalm 86:10). So if during the course of a worship service, the Holy Spirit brings a certain name or attribute of God to mind or prompts you to give thanks, then respond accordingly. That's what Spirit-led worship is all about.

Ponder and Apply

1 During church this week, identify a name or attribute of God that you feel especially drawn to during worship. Afterward, journal about your experience or share your thoughts with someone.

2 Look for an opportunity to give thanks during worship this week. Share afterward what exactly prompted your gratitude.

3 Would those who know you well regard you as predominantly a worshiper or a complainer? Explain.

4 Is there anything more you can do to fend off distractions during the worship service at church this weekend?

5 Write your own personal *dayenu* ("it would have been enough") that tells the story of God's faithfulness to you and your family throughout your life.

FOR PASTORS AND WORSHIP LEADERS

Worship music falls into several categories: call to worship, testimonial, commitment or response, seasonal—just to name a few. Those are all well and good, but my hope is that worship leaders will become increasingly motivated to include songs of pure ascription in worship or write such songs themselves.

At Harvest Bible Chapel we intentionally include at least one song of pure ascription at every service. As we plan the worship set, everything builds to that point when we focus exclusively on God Almighty and reverently proclaim his worth. For many, it's the high point of the service.

Last month, for example, we featured one such song of pure ascription as the offertory special. As the arrangement built toward the end and the worship team kept repeating phrases like "King of Kings and Lord of All; our God is holy," the congregation voluntarily rose to their feet—without any prompting. Many also joined in the singing and raised their hands in worship. When the song ended, we all stood there breathlessly quiet. It was a holy moment, a beautiful, otherworldly type of experience that afforded each of us a glimpse of God's transcendence.

During corporate worship one time, Moses, the great patriarch of Israel, said, "For I will proclaim the name of the LORD; ascribe greatness to our God!" (Deuteronomy 32:3). C. S. Lewis believed: "The perfect church service would be one we were almost unaware of; our attention would have been on God."[41] That's the essence of ascriptive worship, and that's our job as worship leaders: to point people to God in heartfelt worship.

CHAPTER 6

Go All Out
Bring God Your Best Worship

Shanna pulled into the parking lot at Lakeview Community Church and noticed there were no other cars in sight. She glanced at her watch … 6:55. *Oh well*, she thought, *I'm five minutes early.* She tried the front door, but it was locked. She went back to her car and waited. Seven o'clock. She double-checked the name of the church and the address. She was definitely at the right place.

At 7:10, another car pulled up. A young man crawled out carrying a guitar case and moved nonchalantly up the steps to the church. Shanna left her car, strapped on her backpack, and hurried to meet him at the door. "Good morning," the young man said in a friendly tone. "You must be Shanna. My name is Derek. Pleased to meet you."

"Pleased to meet you too," Shanna replied. "You're the Derek who's in charge of the music, right?"

"That's me," Derek said as he unlocked the doors. "Morris said you're the best piano player around. Thanks for playing with us this morning."

"My pleasure." Shanna smiled. "Glad to fill in. Morris told me that rehearsal started at seven, so I was starting to get worried that I had the wrong church or something."

"We're supposed to start at seven," Derek explained, "but it usually doesn't work out that way. You know musicians." They both laughed.

Shanna followed Derek through the lobby and into the sanctuary. He flipped on the lights and Shanna made her way to the piano and started warming up. Shortly after, the drummer, bass player, and sound technician arrived. Around 7:45, Derek got everyone's attention. "I'd like to introduce Shanna to you all," he began. They all said, "Hi," and waved politely at Shanna. "She's filling in for Morris. His grandmother passed away yesterday, so he flew out of town late last night. Let's remember Morris and his family in our prayers."

Everyone nodded in agreement. After a long pause, the bass player cleared his throat and asked, "Do you know what songs we're doing today?"

"No, sorry," Derek replied sheepishly. "I was really busy this week and didn't get time to work up an order."

"How about that new song we talked about a couple weeks ago?" suggested the drummer.

"I haven't had time to learn that yet," put in the bass player. "Let's just do what we did last week."

"I'm tired of those songs," Derek said. "Let's do something different." The discussion continued for about a half hour, but still no decision was reached about what songs to play. Nonetheless, at 8:15 the band went through a routine mic check. At 8:30, one of the ushers arrived with coffee and doughnuts, so Derek told everyone to take a break and meet backstage by ten minutes to nine.

Shanna cornered Derek before he left the platform. "I still don't know what songs we're doing," she pleaded.

"That's okay," Derek said, trying to comfort her. "Just follow me. We'll just play it by ear."

Shanna's eyes lit up. "Will this be like a spontaneous worship time?" she asked excitedly. "You know, free form? Throw out the set list and let the Spirit move? I've always wanted to do a service like that!"

Derek looked puzzled. "No, we're not really into that sort of thing."

"Oh," Shanna said, a little embarrassed. "Well, how will I know what key you're in?"

"Just wing it." Derek smiled. "That's what we usually do."

Discussion Questions

1 Do you feel as though Derek and the worship team are adequately prepared to lead worship this particular Sunday?

2 Do you think the congregation at Lakeview Community Church can tell when their worship team is "winging it"? Why or why not?

3 What kind of impression do you think Shanna formed regarding the worship ministry at Lakeview Community?

4 Do you believe that Derek and the team are bringing God their best efforts in terms of leading worship? Why or why not?

5 As a congregation member, how would you react if the worship team at your church thought nothing of "winging it" on Sunday morning?

Unapologetically Passionate

The most exciting and innovative worship is not happening at the trendiest mega-church in town; it's occurring right now in heaven. Indeed, heavenly worship is lively, fun, and exciting; it is not at all staid or drab. It's an exhilarating, non-stop, joy-filled celebration — the ultimate party — with God's glory on full display. The scene around God's throne is so stunningly breathtaking that John struggles for words to describe it:

> At once I was in the Spirit, and behold, a throne stood in heaven, with one seated on the throne. And he who sat there had the appearance of jasper and carnelian, and around the throne was a rainbow that had the appearance of an emerald. Around the throne were twenty-four thrones, and seated on the thrones were twenty-four elders, clothed in white garments, with golden crowns on their heads. From the throne came flashes of lightning, and rumblings and peals of thunder, and before the throne were burning seven torches of fire, which are the seven spirits of God, and before the throne there was as it were a sea of glass, like crystal.
>
> REVELATION 4:2-6

The glory of God radiates so brilliantly throughout heaven that there is no need for any other source of light: "And the city has no need of sun or moon to shine on it, for the glory of God gives it light, and its lamp is the Lamb" (Revelation 21:23). John Piper asserts, "Heaven will be a never-ending, ever-increasing discovery of more and more of God's glory with greater and ever-greater joy in him."[42]

As you'd expect, worship in heaven is no laid-back affair:

> Then I looked, and I heard around the throne and the living creatures and the elders the voice of many angels, numbering

myriads of myriads and thousands of thousands, saying with a loud voice, "Worthy is the Lamb who was slain, to receive power and wealth and wisdom and might and honor and glory and blessing!" And I heard every creature in heaven and on earth and under the earth and in the sea, and all that is in them, saying, "To him who sits on the throne and to the Lamb be blessing and honor and glory and might forever and ever!" And the four living creatures said, "Amen!" and the elders fell down and worshiped.

REVELATION 5:11–14

Worship in heaven is unapologetically passionate and highly demonstrative. The whole multitude worship God, each with their whole heart. Heaven's worship is also physical. John saw the heavenly host fall on their faces before God:

And all the angels were standing around the throne and around the elders and the four living creatures, and they fell on their faces before the throne and worshiped God.

REVELATION 7:11

And the twenty-four elders who sit on their thrones before God fell on their faces and worshiped God.

REVELATION 11:16

In heaven, humility is the only possible posture, and the glory of God throws the worshipers to their knees. Everyone is actively involved.

Passionate Worship throughout the Bible

Scripture often reports that an individual or a group of people worshiped, but specific details at times are lacking. I've always wondered what exactly they did when they worshiped. For example, we are told in Nehemiah 9:3 that the people of Israel worshiped, but we're not told how. Did they spontaneously break into a few praise choruses? Did they recite Scripture? Did they pray? What exactly did they do?

I recently spent several days looking up all the verses in the Bible that use the word "worship" in order to gain some insight into worship practices of the Jews and the early church. The more I probed, the more I realized that those in Scripture worshiped God with great passion. In the Old Testament, the original Hebrew word used most often for worship means to bow down, fall down, humbly beseech, do reverence.[43] The Greek word for worship used most often in the New Testament has similar meaning: to prostrate oneself in homage, do reverence to, adore.[44] These words are physical. Reading them in context bears this out. In Exodus 34:8, we are told that Moses "bowed his head toward the earth and worshiped." Job "fell on the ground and worshiped" (Job 1:20). The disciples took hold of Jesus' feet and worshiped him (Matthew 28:9). The people of Israel "bowed down with their faces to the ground on the pavement and worshiped" (2 Chronicles 7:3). In 2 Chronicles 20:18, we learn that "Jehoshaphat bowed his head with his face to the ground, and all Judah and the inhabitants of Jerusalem fell down before the LORD, worshiping the LORD" (see also Exodus 12:27; 1 Chronicles 29:20; 2 Chronicles 29:30). In the Bible, people don't sit passively in pews during worship. They get passionately and physically involved.

Heaven's Cure for Our Complacency

Most of us are much more inhibited in our worship than our spiritual forefathers in Scripture. Maybe we're quiet and reserved by nature. Or perhaps we grew up in a church that stressed restraint. I have a friend who blames his stoic expression during corporate worship on his constrained Scandinavian heritage. He sings softly but with no visible expression or energy. I don't doubt my friend's sincerity, but heaven's standard for worship is much more effusive than that.

It is simply unnatural to restrain our worship. It's human nature to exude joy and energy. We get visibly exercised over a new car, a good meal, or our favorite movie. When discussing sports, religion, or politics, many of us are very animated; we use our hands to emphasize certain words or phrases. When we speak about a loved one, our eyes light up, we smile; our feet may even bounce as if they're about to break into dance. I don't know anyone who speaks in constant monotone, with no facial expression, hands glued to their sides when talking about something or someone they love. Yet that's how some of us try to worship. Meanwhile the saints in heaven are doing face plants in homage to the King of Kings.

So why do we hold back? Why so reticent? Why do we settle for lackluster worship?

Culturally Conditioned

Modern churchgoers are culturally conditioned to be comfortable and complacent, instead of actively engaged, during worship. We live in an entertainment-driven world. We flip on TV, radio, computer, or iPod and these modern miracles of technology ask nothing of us but to sit back and enjoy. We "veg out," escaping into a world where we don't have to think, act, or do anything but relax and take it all in. There's nothing wrong with entertainment per se, but when it dominates our lives, it produces a bystander mentality, where we observe life from a distance without getting actively involved. Worship has become a spectator sport.

Unfortunately, too many of us approach church the same way —as casual observers instead of active participants. We come to watch the choir or worship team and listen to the music. We'll join in and sing here and there but we mostly hang back, as if we're spectators observing a performance. We act more like outsiders and newcomers than God's loved children. We plop down in the pew and wait for somebody to tell us what to do. The result is lethargic worship.

Pride

Sometimes pride prevents us from fully entering into worship. We want to avoid looking foolish, weak, or awkward because it might tarnish our image or damage our reputation. When David brought the ark of the covenant to Jerusalem, the people celebrated and David danced "with all his might ... wearing a linen ephod" (2 Samuel 6:14). Second Samuel 6:16 informs us that he was "leaping and dancing before the LORD." This was no stately or well-choreographed promenade. Imagine David wildly flailing away in his skivvies. Michal, David's wife, was thoroughly embarrassed and later chided her husband for his raucous celebration, which she contended was unbecoming for a king. Note David's response: "It was before the LORD ... and I will make merry before the LORD. I will make myself yet more contemptible than this" (2 Samuel 6:21–22). David was saying, "I don't care how undignified it looks. I'm not going to hold back when it comes time to worship. In fact, I would gladly look even more undignified if it brought glory to God."

Often it's the prideful person who says, "God knows my heart. I don't have to sing, bow, kneel, or raise my hands to prove I love him." That may sound spiritual, but most of the time it's an excuse. If we truly believed that God knows our hearts, we'd realize that he can also tell when we're being prideful and arrogant. Actions always accompany heartfelt convictions. "The good person out of the good treasure of his heart produces good, and the evil person out of his evil treasure produces evil" (Luke 6:45). Jesus also said, "Everyone who acknowledges me before men, the Son of Man also will acknowledge before the angels of God, but the one who denies me before men will be denied before the angels of God" (Luke 12:8–9). It is a shame to permit pride to keep you from publicly proclaiming through worship that you are a follower of Christ, that you belong to Jesus, and he is Lord of your life.

Fear of Others

Some of us are afraid of what others might think if they saw us fervently worshiping God. We fear their disapproval, maybe even their scorn. The apostle John reports that in Jesus' day, "many even of the authorities believed in him, but for fear of the Pharisees they did not confess it, so that they would not be put out of the synagogue; for they loved the glory that comes from man more than the glory that comes from God" (John 12:42–43). First Thessalonians 2:4 teaches that our goal in life should be "not to

TAKEAWAY #6:

Bring God Your Best Worship

Though heavenly worship is bold, passionate, and physical, I wouldn't get hung up on externals, like the Pharisees did. You never want to manufacture passion or make worship all about you and your perceived performance. Ultimately, it doesn't matter whether you sit, stand, bow, raise hands, or kneel to worship. Those are outward manifestations of an inward passion for God. What does matter is that you bring God your best worship.

please man, but to please God." If you fear what others think, it's time to ask whether the approval of others is more important to you than God's approval. For in the final analysis, we worship before an audience of One.

That's typically what David did; he brought God his best worship. One time David wanted to honor the Lord with a special sacrifice and a man named Araunah offered to provide for free all the materials needed to build the appropriate altar. However, David politely declined, saying that he didn't want to offer the Lord that which cost him nothing (2 Samuel 24:24). David didn't want to give God halfhearted worship.

Jesus commands us to "love the Lord your God with *all* your heart and with *all* your soul and with *all* your mind and with *all* your strength" (Mark 12:30, emphasis added). We are to worship the Lord enthusiastically and completely, with everything we've got.

Bringing God our best worship may mean something different for each of us, depending on personality, temperament, and religious background. For example, if your personality is quiet, laid back, or reserved, bringing God your best worship might mean that you do something overt, like raise your hands or kneel. If you're an extrovert, you might at times want to consider sitting reverently still in God's presence during corporate worship. As you try to discern what it means to bring God your best worship, I humbly offer what I hope are a few helpful suggestions.

Come Hungry for God

First, come to church hungry for God. The psalmist wrote, "As a deer pants for flowing streams, so pants my soul for you, O God. My soul thirsts for God, for the living God. When shall I come and appear before God?" (Psalm 42:1 – 2). Notice that the writer is not only hungry for God but is eager to "come" to the place where God's people worship him. John Piper wrote:

> The basic movement of worship on Sunday morning is not to come with our hands full to give to God, as though he needed anything (Acts 17:25), but to come with our hands empty, to receive from God. And what we receive in worship is the fullness of God, not the feelings of entertainment. We ought to come hungry for God.... God is mightily honored when a people know that they will die of hunger and thirst unless they have God.
>
> Nothing makes God more supreme and more central in worship than when a people are utterly persuaded that nothing—not money or prestige or leisure or family or job or health or sports or toys or friends—nothing is going to bring satisfaction to their sinful, guilty, aching hearts besides God. This conviction breeds a people who go hard after God on Sunday morning. They are not confused about why they are in a worship service. They do not view songs and prayers and sermons as mere traditions or mere duties. They see them as means of getting to God or God getting to them for more of his fullness—no matter how painful that may be for sinners in the short run.[45]

Walk into church raring to go. Come eager to encounter God. Respond to his presence with the praise and worship he deserves.

Come Ready to Contribute

God's Word teaches that the body of Christ works best when we all contribute. "When you come together, each one has a hymn, a lesson, a revelation, a tongue, or an interpretation. Let all things be done for building up" (1 Corinthians 14:26). Instead of being casual observers, we are to come to church every Sunday ready and willing to contribute.

Liturgical churches perhaps understand better than others that worship is participatory. The word *liturgy* comes from a Greek word that originally meant "the work of the people." Worship, therefore, is something we all do together to honor God. Worship is not passive, but calls forth effort from every one of us. There is a little bit of work involved. It's called a worship *service*. Worship, therefore, is not something done for us or that we watch others do; it is something we do for God.

Make Your Praise Visible

If you come to church willing to contribute, you won't sit back like a bump on a log; you'll automatically engage during worship. When God specified his design for the tabernacle, he made no mention of chairs. The Israelites worshiped on their feet the entire time. If you are elderly or disabled, you may not be able to stand for long periods (and that's okay), but we are all called to be physically involved, to the extent that you're able, during worship — to "glorify God in your body" (1 Corinthians 6:20).

Physical expressions of worship include standing, kneeling, bowing, raising hands, and clapping. While I would never suggest you do anything that feels forced or violates your conscience, I do recommend getting physically involved in some way as you worship. Scripture allows for a great deal of freedom in this area, but I would also caution against doing anything inappropriate or disruptive. Avoid calling undue attention to yourself. The apostle Paul stipulated that corporate worship "be done decently and in order" (1 Corinthians 14:40). Always have good reason for your actions. There is significant meaning behind every physical gesture or posture mentioned in the Bible.

Standing, Kneeling, Bowing

Standing is appropriate for paying tribute or showing honor. Nehemiah reports that when Ezra read God's Word, the people stood out of respect (Nehemiah 8:5). They also stood during worship (Nehemiah 9:5; see also Exodus 33:10; 2 Chronicles 20:19).

Kneeling and bowing are postures of submission. Philippians 2:10 announces that "at the name of Jesus every knee should bow, in heaven and on earth and under the earth" (see also Psalm 95:6; 138:2; Matthew 17:14). Pastor Mark Roberts points out that "the Psalms *never* encourage us to sit in worship. God alone sits upon his throne as we assume the postures of servanthood either standing or bowing before him."[46]

Raising Hands, Clapping

Raising hands is a typical posture for prayer and worship in the Bible (see Psalm 141:2). Though some may be uncomfortable raising hands, the Bible clearly invites all serious worshipers to do so. "Lift up your hands to the holy place and bless the LORD!" (Psalm 134:2; see also 1 Timothy 2:8). Personally, I find lifting my hands helps direct my attention heavenward to the Lord, as Psalm 63:4 illustrates: "So I will bless you as long as I live; in your name I will lift up my hands." Worshipers may also raise hands to emphasize a line from a song or prayer, like saying "Amen" when you hear something with which you strongly agree. A good example is found in Nehemiah 8:6: "And Ezra blessed the LORD, the great God, and all the people answered, 'Amen, Amen,' lifting up their hands." Some lift up their hands to express their need for God. David cried out, "Hear the voice of my pleas for mercy, when I cry to you for help, when I lift up my hands toward your most holy sanctuary" (Psalm 28:2; see also 88:8–9). Raising hands can also signify dependence or submission. Lamentations 3:40–41 says,

"Let us test and examine our ways, and return to the LORD! Let us lift up our hearts and hands to God in heaven." If you're shy about raising your hands in worship, start out with small, simple gestures, like holding your palms open in front of you. As you grow more comfortable, you can always raise your hands higher.

Clapping is also sanctioned by the Bible, but make sure you're clear about why you're doing it. When appropriate, it's okay to clap after a song or sermon. That's a common way to express appreciation. However, Scripture proposes a higher purpose for clapping: to joyously celebrate God. "Clap your hands, all peoples! Shout to God with loud songs of joy!" (Psalm 47:1).

Save Your Best for God

What would it look like for you to make your worship visible? If you're normally shy and unassuming, what does it look like for you to worship God passionately? How much physical expression is enough? How much is too much?

Here's a simple guideline: you should exert more energy worshiping God than you do cheering for your favorite sports team, your kid's soccer team, or your favorite band. Even if you're not a sports fan or you don't attend rock concerts, I think you get the point. Your countenance and your posture should visibly demonstrate that you mean business when it comes to worshiping God.

I'm fairly quiet by nature, but you'd never know it if you saw me at a baseball game. I'm a die-hard Chicago White Sox fan. In rooting for my team, I've been known to stand, clap, jump up and down, whoop, and holler. Not all of those actions are reverent enough for church, but I know I need to worship God with more intensity and energy than I do when cheering for the Sox. When you worship, make sure God doesn't get shortchanged; always give him your best.

Make Your Praise Audible

Psalm 66:8 points out that worship must also be audible: "Bless our God, O peoples; let the sound of his praise be heard." David saw no reason to remain tight-lipped when it came time for corporate worship:

> I have told the glad news of deliverance in the great congregation; behold, I have not restrained my lips, as you know, O LORD. I have not hidden your deliverance within my heart; I have spoken of your faithfulness and your salvation; I have not concealed your steadfast love and your faithfulness from the great congregation.
>
> PSALM 40:9–10

David can't keep quiet about all that the Lord has done for him.

Hebrews 13:15 contends that our worship is to be "the fruit of lips that acknowledge his name." And in heaven, God's praise is routinely spoken (Revelation 4:8–11; 11:16–17), shouted (Revelation 5:11–14; 7:10; 19:1–3), and sung.

Do I Really Have to Sing?

A good friend of mine heard that I was writing a book about worship in heaven and she shared that her husband's first question would be: "Do I have to sing in heaven?" He's hoping the answer is no, because he doesn't like to sing. In spite of my friend's reluctance, there will be plenty of singing in heaven. Check out Revelation 5:9, 14:3, and 15:3 to see what I mean. I have a hard time imagining anyone in heaven saying, "I'll take a pass and sit this one out." We'll all want to join in and sing!

The Bible also clearly commands us to sing: "Sing praises to God, sing praises! Sing praises to ... the King of all the earth; sing praises with a psalm!" (Psalm 47:6–7; see also Psalm 68:4, 32). In Psalm 100:2, we are told to come into God's presence with singing. You can't be a serious worshiper and refuse to sing. If you love the Lord and you're grateful for the blessings you've received, why wouldn't you want to sing his praises at the top of your lungs? David proclaimed, "I will sing to the LORD, because he has dealt bountifully with me" (Psalm 13:6). James wrote, "Is anyone cheerful? Let him sing praise" (James 5:13). You don't have to love music to worship God; you just have to love Jesus.

If you're not keen on singing, let's first of all dispel the notion that one has to be an accomplished singer to worship. Writing in the eighteenth century, William Law reasons accordingly:

> You will perhaps say, that singing is a particular talent, that belongs only to particular people, and that you have neither voice nor ear to make any music.
>
> If you had said that singing is a general talent, and that people differ in that as they do in all other things, you had said something much truer.
>
> For how vastly do people differ in the talent of thinking.... Yet no one desires to be excused from thought, or reason, or discourse.... So it is singing, and not artful, fine singing, that is a required way of praising God.[47]

Nowhere in the Bible is it even hinted that one must be a bona fide singer to effectively worship God. God looks at your heart, not at how well you sing.

One of my more embarrassing moments occurred while on a mission trip to the Dominican Republic. Upon landing in Santo Domingo, I was eager to make a good first impression by greeting our Dominican hosts in friendly fashion. Everyone knows that "Hello" in Spanish is "¡Hola!" Yet, for some reason, I went up to the first person I saw, extended my hand and said "Aloha!" My new friend looked at me as if I had gotten off the wrong boat, then laughed and shook my hand. I continued to muddle my way through the rest of the trip, employing a crafty mix of English, remedial Spanish, and word pictures. I noticed that whether I spoke Spanglish or fluent Hawaiian, my hosts seemed to appreciate my primitive efforts to connect with them.

In the same way, no matter how badly you sing, God appreciates the effort. If you at least try to sing, God will honor the intentions of your heart. But if you make no attempt at all, you're in effect telling God that he's not worth the effort. Better to sing God's praise off-key than not to sing at all.

And, men, don't fall for the notion that singing is somehow "womanly." King David was a warrior, a real "man's man," but he was also a poet and singer. Jesus and his burly band of disciples sang a hymn as they left the upper room (Matthew 26:30). If Jesus is not above singing, then neither should you and I be. Furthermore, Zephaniah 3:17 divulges that God himself sings: "The LORD your God is in your midst.... He will exult over you with loud singing." So singing is not just for women; real men boldly sing God's praise.

Make a Joyful Noise

If you really can't carry a tune, at least you can make what Scripture refers to as a "joyful noise." Psalm 95:1–2 says, "Oh come, let us sing to the LORD; let us make a joyful noise to the rock of our salvation! Let us come into his presence with thanksgiving; let us make a joyful noise to him with songs of praise!" (see also Psalm 98:4, 6; 100:1). Making a joyful noise sets the bar within everyone's reach. You can sing monotone, be tone deaf, or have the worst voice in the world, but if your heart's on fire for God, your singing is music to his ears. Don't hold back. Sing out! For some of you, bringing God your best worship might mean that you make more of an effort to sing or, if need be, that you offer him your unique version of that "joyful noise."

Feelings Are Okay

If you're a "thinker" and you tend to be cerebral, bringing God your best worship may mean that you allow yourself to be a little more emotional during worship. Remember, Jesus commanded, "You shall love the Lord your God with all your *heart* and with all your *soul* and with all your *strength* and with all your *mind*" (Luke 10:27, emphasis added). Worship is meant to be holistic, combining the cognitive, physical, and emotional. David exclaimed, "I will sing and make melody with all my being!" (Psalm 108:1).

A. W. Tozer insists that worship that doesn't include both thoughts and feelings is incomplete:

> I have had people tell me very dogmatically that they will never allow "feeling" to have any part in their spiritual life and experience. I reply, "Too bad for you!" I say that because I have voiced a very real definition of what I believe true worship to be: *worship is to feel in the heart!*
>
> In the Christian faith, we should be able to use the word "feel" boldly and without apology. What worse thing could be said of us as the Christian church if it could be said that we are a feelingless people?[48]

Suppressing feelings only stifles worship. Ephesians 5:19 exhorts us to sing and make music to the Lord "with your heart." The psalmist wrote, "My heart and flesh sing for joy to the living God" (Psalm 84:2). Singing opens you up to your emotions and helps you express your deepest feelings for God.

Sing to Someone

If you want to grow as a singing worshiper, always sing to someone. Colossians 3:16 invites all to "let the word of Christ dwell in you richly, teaching and admonishing *one another* in all wisdom, singing psalms and hymns and spiritual songs, with thankfulness in your hearts *to God*" (emphasis added). Whenever we sing in worship, we do so with a view to God and/or each other. Some songs emphasize our relationship to God, such as "Be Thou My Vision," "Change My Heart, O God," and "As the Deer." Some refer to these as "vertical" songs. Other songs are "horizontal." They're sung about God but to each other—to encourage and edify fellow believers. Examples include "All Hail the Power of Jesus' Name," "Crown Him with Many Crowns," and "To God Be the Glory."

It's important to identify to whom you are singing because it will affect how you worship. If singing directly to the Lord, you might want to lift your gaze and/or your arms heavenward. Or you may want to open your hands, palms up, to signify the offering of yourself to God or that you're open to receive from him. You may even choose to bow or kneel. Or you may just want to prayerfully close your eyes as you sing.

On the other hand, when singing to fellow believers, you may want to fix your gaze lower, to those sitting around you or to face a part of the congregation seated farther away. You may want to sing in the direction of someone seated nearby who's hurting and needs a word of encouragement. Similarly, a line of a song may remind you to pray for someone in need. Recently during worship at my church, we sang a song that spoke of God as our Healer. It was just one line, but it caught my ear. I immediately thought of two friends who are battling prostate cancer, and I sang the line as if they were standing next to me. I also said a brief prayer on their behalf.

There are also times when you may need to be sung to. If you're going through difficulty, consider being silent while being reminded of God's grace, power, and love. Let the Holy Spirit use the words of the songs to minister to you.

Sing What You Mean and Mean What You Sing

Worship is serious business, so be careful never to sing anything you don't mean. In 1 Corinthians 14:15, Paul says, "I will sing praise with my spirit, but I will sing *with my mind* also" (emphasis added). Don't just sing words. Think about what you're singing.

There's a line from a song we sing at my church that tells the Lord, "You're my everything." Before singing that, I have to ask, "Is that really true of me? Is God everything to me? Is he really all I need to be happy, content, and fulfilled?" I don't want to sing anything I don't mean (and I bet you don't either). Mean what you sing and sing what you mean.

God Deserves Our Best

In conclusion, if you want to experience worship on earth as it is in heaven, come to church hungry for God, come ready to contribute, making your praise visible and audible. Bring God your best worship. In Malachi 1:14, the Lord admonishes the nation of Israel because they weren't bringing their best sacrifices to the altar. Instead of putting forth their best cattle, sheep, or goats, the people would offer blemished animals, ones that were sick, old, or lame. It doesn't honor God when we bring him less than our best.

After all, God has always given us his best. He created a world that, even in its fallen state, captivates us with its beauty and grandeur. When God rolled out the plan of salvation, he again gave us his best — he sent his only begotten Son. At this moment, Jesus is preparing a place for you in paradise. When you get to heaven, it won't be like checking into a fine hotel. It'll be more like coming home to a place custom built, specially designed — for you — by Christ himself! God has always gone out of his way for you, so don't hold back when it comes to praising him. Always bring God your best worship — he certainly deserves it.

Ponder and Apply

1 What does it mean for you personally to bring God your best worship?

2 How can you make your worship more visible and/or more audible?

3 How can someone who doesn't like to sing engage meaningfully in worship?

4 What role, if any, should emotions play in worship?

5 What can you do to participate more fully during corporate worship at church next weekend?

FOR PASTORS AND WORSHIP LEADERS

Nowhere is the old adage "speed of the leader, speed of the team" more applicable than in the area of worship. In most churches, it's the pastor, even more than the worship leader, who sets the tone for the entire congregation. Everyone in the congregation knows where the pastor sits during the service and notices whether or not he or she participates during worship. It's no coincidence that churches known for their vibrant worship also have pastors who worship openly and freely.

We worship leaders also need to consistently bring God our best worship. In contrast to the worship team in the opening scenario of this chapter, let's make sure we plan prayerfully, rehearse adequately, and prepare spiritually in order to effectively lead God's people in worship.

The Old Testament describes a worship service under King

Hezekiah in which the leaders, the Levites and priests, "praised the LORD day by day, singing with all their might to the LORD" (2 Chronicles 30:21). That's a good example for us leaders to follow. If you want your congregation to bring God their best worship, make sure you, as pastor and/or worship leader, are setting the pace.

To help the congregation engage during worship, it's a good idea to remind the people from time to time the reason behind our methods. I grew up in the Lutheran church and experienced its liturgy every week. As a young person, I found the service painfully boring. Later in life, I attended a workshop that unveiled the meaning behind the various parts of a Lutheran worship service. I learned that the Introit is basically a call to worship and that the Kyrie is placed near the beginning of the service so the congregation can come into God's presence with humble, repentant hearts. I gained a whole new respect and appreciation for liturgy, as well as the church calendar, that continues to this day.

Don't assume that everyone in the congregation knows why you do what you do. Even informal churches have their forms and routines. From time to time, guide your people through a specific part of the service. Take the time to describe your church's philosophy of worship. Tell them why you do the type of music you do. Explain any rituals, customs, or traditions, especially those unique to your fellowship. Describe the meaning behind any symbols such as the altar, candles, vestments, or colors. Share the stories behind the writing of your church's favorite hymns or praise choruses. Your people will participate more fully when they understand the spiritual significance behind each part of the service.

CHAPTER 7

Welcome All Ages
Set Aside Personal Preferences

When Christina was asked to chair the worship planning committee at her church, she could hardly contain herself. It was her dream job, although it would have been dreamier had she been paid. No matter. Christina had a passion for worship, a wealth of ideas, and loads of energy. She was more than happy to volunteer for the job.

The night of her first meeting, Christina arrived at church early, set up two flip charts, a whiteboard, a portable CD player, and a table with five chairs. She scattered markers, sticky notes, and candy across the table. She read somewhere that the secret to leading successful brainstorming meetings is to provide plenty of sweets.

Everyone arrived early. *That's a good sign!* Christina thought. After opening in prayer and sharing a few Bible verses, Christina invited everyone to share their ideas. "Let's fill these flip charts with the most creative ideas our church has ever seen!" she exclaimed. Silence. "No idea is a bad idea," she prodded. "Who wants to start?" Still nothing.

Becky, middle-aged mother of three, finally let out a hearty laugh and said, "We thought we were coming to hear your ideas." Everyone smiled and laughed.

"Yeah, Pastor Phil said you're the most creative young lady he's ever met," added Morgan, a cheerful, silver-haired retiree. "I've been looking forward to this meeting for months."

"Me too," chimed in Jason, "but I didn't know we were supposed to bring anything." Jason is a college student who plays guitar and sings on the worship team.

Next to him sat Odessa, real estate agent and the church's best female vocalist. "Honey, this committee has been meeting for over a year," said Odessa, "and we haven't accomplished a single thing. We need you to lead us."

"Well, I did bring a few ideas," Christina began with a gleam in her eye. "For starters, I brought a praise song I heard at a conference last week that's one of the best songs I've heard in a long time. I've got it cued up and ready to go." She enthusiastically passed out lyric sheets and, as the sound of pulsating electric guitars filled the room, Christina closed her eyes and sang along.

When the song ended, Christina looked up, eyebrows raised. "What do you think?" she asked expectantly.

Silence again.

Jason cleared his throat. "I'm not really into that mainstream stuff," he said. "I like indie music myself."

"Oh, I do too," Christina replied, undaunted, "but I need to remind us that we're here to choose music that's best for the congregation, not just for ourselves."

Morgan looked puzzled. "What's indie music?"

Odessa rolled her eyes. "It's not really music," she said. "Just four chords that drone on forever and no melody to speak of."

"It's got depth," Jason shot back.

"I for one would be disappointed if we started playing indie-type music in church," Odessa continued. "I'd quit coming, that's for sure. And, Christina, I didn't much care for that song you played either. What do you all think about us starting a gospel choir?"

Several nodded in agreement. Christina picked up on their sudden energy. "That's a great idea, Odessa. Do you know anyone who could lead it?"

"Well, I would, honey, if I had the time!" Odessa said. They all laughed.

"I brought a song," Becky said, eagerly reaching for her purse. "It's an older song—"

"Don't tell me," Jason cut in. "It's from the eighties, right?"

Becky looked hurt. "It's my all-time favorite song. We used to sing it here all the time."

Odessa looked straight at Christina. "We get into this argument all the time."

"What do you mean?" Christina asked.

"About what we *used* to do at the church," Odessa said. "It's a real sore spot for Morgan."

"Well, our church used to have a top-notch music program," Morgan said angrily. "We had a huge choir, handbells, and the biggest pipe organ in the state. Now most of those old choir people have left the church, and that organ just sits there gathering dust. It's a shame. After all I've done for this church and all the money I've given, is it too much to ask to hear the blasted pipe organ once in a while?"

Jason pulled away from the table and spoke in a low but serious tone. "If we bring back choir, organ, and the music of the seventies and eighties, there's no reason for me to stick around here any longer."

At that point, Becky burst into tears. Christina looked at Odessa and whispered, "Is this normal?"

"Oh, honey, we're on our best behavior tonight. You should see us on a bad day."

Christina walked over to Becky, put her arm around her, and offered some tissues. Then she slowly looked around the table. "Let's call it a night. We'll pick up again next week."

Discussion Questions

1 What advice do you have for Christina as she continues to lead this committee?

2 What advice do you have for each committee member as they move forward from here?

3 Assuming that each committee person's opinion represents a percentage of the congregation, what are some of the controversies you think this church might be facing in regard to its worship services?

4 What are some of the interrelational obstacles this group needs to overcome in order to work well together?

5 What do you think about people who threaten to leave their church if the style of music doesn't suit them? Is it justified? Why or why not?

Heaven's Worship Is Intergenerational

In heaven, we will worship with all the believers who have gone before us as well as those yet to come. Jesus foretold that we will rub shoulders "with Abraham, Isaac, and Jacob in the kingdom of heaven" (Matthew 8:11). Imagine singing God's praise alongside Moses, David, Peter, James, John, Paul, Augustine, Francis of Assisi, Martin Luther, John Wesley, John Calvin, Charles Spurgeon, D. L. Moody, C. S. Lewis, and Mother Teresa. In heaven, you will not find separate services for each age group. Generations past, present, and future will come together to worship.

Intergenerational Worship throughout Scripture

Psalm 148:12 – 13 paints a vivid picture of young and old worshiping together: "Young men and maidens together, old men and children! Let them praise the name of the LORD." Scripture invites all ages to witness to each other about the glory of the Lord. "One generation shall commend your works to another, and shall declare your mighty acts" (Psalm 145:4). Ephesians 3:21 reminds us that no particular age group has cornered the market on worship, but that God will be glorified "in the church and in Christ Jesus throughout all generations, forever and ever. Amen."

Where Are All the Twenty-Year-Olds?

Though well supported throughout Scripture, intergenerational worship has been supplanted by strictly defined age-segregated services in most churches today. Whether they're called traditional, contemporary, blended, next-gen, or some other trendy moniker, the options are often drawn along generational lines. This approach has done more to polarize the generations than bring them together.

Today's church is failing to reach the twentysomething age group. According to a recent survey conducted by the Barna Research Group, only 33 percent of twenty-year-olds attend church in a typical week.[49] That is the lowest attendance figure of any age group. The Southern Baptist Convention reports that 88 percent of the children raised in Christian homes leave church by the age of eighteen and never return.[50] A recent article in *Time* magazine estimated that 61 percent of twenty-year-olds who were involved at church during their teen years no longer attend.[51] In a 2007 survey, Lifeway Research reported that 70 percent of young adults ages 23 – 30 stopped attending church regularly for at least a year while in their late teens and early twenties.[52]

Statistics prove what many are observing: today's twenty-year-olds are opting out of church at an alarming rate. As I travel, visiting various churches, I can't help but notice the lack of young adults in attendance. On two occasions, pastors told me that they tried earnestly to attract more twentysomethings to church, but it didn't work. They gave up. I certainly don't disparage them for giving up; at least they tried. The statistics don't lie. Churches that host an event for young adults during the week are having a tough time getting those same young people to church on Sunday. Even churches that offer a Saturday evening "next-gen" service are having a difficult time getting those young people to assimilate into the life of the church. Many mega-churches that flourished in the 1980s and '90s are now aging congregations, struggling to reach today's younger generation.

Given this sad state of affairs, I believe that intergenerational worship, more than age-segregated services, has greater potential to bring the twenty-year-olds back to church. Allow me to explain.

Intergenerational Worship— The Time Is Ripe

Today's church is trying to reach basically four generations of adults:

1. Builders (born 1900–1945)

2. Boomers (born 1946–1964)

3. Busters (born 1965–1983)

4. Millennials (born 1984–)

Each generation is distinct, with its own shared experiences, ideologies, and preferences. One generation's values are often formed as a reaction to those of the previous group. My generation rejected what we perceived as our parents' stilted and stodgy approach to church. We wanted services that were more personal, informal, and relevant to everyday life. Today's young adults prefer worship that is less "slick," polished, and performance-oriented than what they see from my generation. Every generation is unique and puts its own characteristic stamp on worship.

Intergenerational worship has the potential not only to bring the twenty-year-olds back to church but also to unify different age groups at the same time. In Romans 15:5–6, Paul exhorts us to "live in such harmony with one another, in accord with Christ Jesus, that together you may with one voice glorify the God and Father of our Lord Jesus Christ." There is no "generation gap" in God's kingdom. Whenever the generations worship together, it is a vivid demonstration of Christian unity.

Malachi 4:6, the last verse of the Old Testament, predicts a day when the hearts of fathers would be turned to their children, and the hearts of children returned to their fathers. The prophet Joel envisioned a time when the Lord would pour out his Spirit, and sons and daughters would prophesy, old men dream dreams, and young men see visions (Joel 2:28). On the day of Pentecost, Peter announced that Joel's prophecy had been fulfilled (Acts 2:16–17). In effect, Peter was saying, "Now is the time for all people, young and old, to come together in the body of Christ." The same could be said of our day. The time is ripe for the generations to join forces, to pull together under the inspiration of the Holy Spirit to do great things for God. In fact, I believe the conditions are currently ripe for intergenerational worship to become not only a salient feature but also a driving force in today's church. My optimism results from the common ground we all share in Christ as well as the openness I sense from the younger generation. I spend a great deal of time mentoring young leaders in their twenties and thirties. The majority of them are serious about following Christ. That's why I'm very encouraged about the future of the church; I believe it's in capable hands. There are five reasons why I believe conditions are favorable for the generations to come together in worship.

REASON #1: *Busters and Millennials Are Open to Having Older People Around*

The next generations value the company and wisdom of older people. They don't want us older folks to run everything, but they don't want us to leave. They want us around. They value our presence and wisdom. That's a far cry from the attitude we Boomers used to have. When my generation was young, our mantra was that we didn't trust anyone over thirty years old. The generations after us, on the other hand, don't trust anyone under thirty when seeking real life wisdom.

A few years ago, I taught a class at Wheaton College on spiritual formation for artists. Toward the end of each class, we broke into small groups and prayed for each other. Before the semester was out, every one of those students voiced the same prayer request for a mentor. I have since found this desire for an older confidant to be typical of young people these days. They value guidance and counsel from their elders.

REASON #2: *Busters and Millennials Are Open to Old Ideas and Ancient Practices*

The next generations appreciate the value of old writings and ancient rituals. They respect time-honored prayers, liturgies, and creeds. They're much more open to using hymns than my generation was when we were their age. They don't want a steady diet of old music, and they'll perform hymns in a contemporary style. But they're smart enough to realize that certain forms and practices have withstood the test of time because they are based on foundational Christian truths and are, therefore, relevant and substantive.

For fun, sometimes I'll pull out a reading from the Book of Common Prayer on a retreat. Whenever I mention that a particular prayer is one that Christians have been praying for several hundred years, I notice all the young people in the room perk up. Most of them are hearing this prayer or liturgy for the first time; the words are completely new to them. Afterward, some even ask where they can find the prayer written by "that old dude." Young people these days are fascinated by long-established spiritual writings and practices.

REASON #3: *Busters and Millennials Are Open to a Wide Variety of Musical Styles*

Today's world offers a smorgasbord of choices, especially when it comes to music. As a result, Busters and Millennials freely embrace a wide variety of musical styles. They're up on the latest indie hits, but they're also surprisingly knowledgeable about classic rock and Motown. When my older son discovered the Beatles, they quickly became his favorite rock group. For the first time in his young life, his dad was cool because I owned several Beatles albums, the covers of which are now nicely framed and adorn the walls of my son's apartment.

What makes intergenerational worship such an exciting possibility is that today's "pop" music is not drastically different from yesterday's. The gap between the music of my generation and that of our children and grandchildren is not nearly as wide as the gap between the music of my generation and that of our parents. The Builder generation loves big band jazz, Broadway musicals, and old revival songs. That's a far cry from the rock music that most Boomers, Busters, and Millennials have grown up with. Granted, when you break it down, "pop" music over the last fifty years has changed and evolved, but the prototypical band is still a rhythm section comprised of drums, bass, guitar, and some kind of keyboard. The snare drum still hits mostly on beats two and four. Male vocalists who are featured sing in their upper registers so as to cut through the electric guitars and keyboards. So three generations are still listening to basically the same genre of music.

In the church today, worship songs are cutting across generational lines like never before. For example, songs recorded by the likes of Chris Tomlin, David Crowder, Darlene Zschech, and Hillsong United are sung not only in church on Sunday but also by the youth group and college-age ministry. When it comes to musical style, the generations enjoy more common ground today than most people realize.

REASON #4: *Busters and Millennials Value Authenticity*

Authenticity is a high value for Busters and Millennials. They quickly sniff out anything that doesn't look, sound, or feel authentic. This is why young adults are turned off by church services that come off as too staged or polished. It doesn't feel "real" to them. As a young songwriter, I remember being told by my pastor never to write a worship song in a minor key. That would have been too much of a "downer." Today's young worship leaders wouldn't think twice about singing a tune in a minor key or embracing songs of lament. Those are authentic responses to life's adversities and, therefore, highly appropriate for worship.

A friend of mine has a twenty-five-year-old son who recently visited a liturgical church in town. My friend asked his son's opinion of the worship service. The first thing the young man said was that the congregation didn't sound like they really believed the Scriptures and creeds they recited. Notice that he wasn't turned off by their traditional approach. He was turned off by their lack of authenticity.

REASON #5: *Busters and Millennials Value Community*

Busters and Millennials place a high value on community. Instead of a large mega-church, many are attracted to smaller, intimate congregations or even house churches. They don't think of church as a building or a service; they think of it as the place where their friends are. They may not always choose a church based on the quality of the worship or teaching. Relationships are more important than programs. That's why the twentysomethings with whom I interact don't want age-segregated services. They prefer a diverse mix of ages and ethnicities because that's a more accurate picture of true community. After all, Psalm 90:1 says that the Lord has been "our dwelling place in all generations."

What Might Intergenerational Worship Look Like for Us Today?

Intergenerational worship is not a new idea; it's clearly sanctioned by Scripture. So what might it look like for today's church? First, when I talk about intergenerational worship, I'm not referring to "blended" worship, which came into vogue during the 1990s. The purpose of blended worship is to offer "something for everyone," yet all too often it yields nothing substantial for anyone.

Second, as a proponent of intergenerational worship, I'm not necessarily suggesting that school-age children be forced to sit through entire church services every week. Some churches, like the Orthodox tradition, encourage the entire family, including young children, to sit together throughout the service. Other churches allow children to sit in the service until the sermon, at which point they depart for Sunday school classes. Both of these approaches hold merit, but they may not be practical or even preferable for every church. What I'm proposing is that we create services that encourage adults, from high school or college age on up, to participate. That is still diametrically opposed to the simultaneous age-segregated services that are the current rage throughout evangelicalism.

A Younger Look with an Older Presence

Many people want to know what this new intergenerational worship sounds like, which assumes I'm describing a particular style of music. That is not the case. Every church needs to determine for itself what musical styles are appropriate for its corporate worship. I can't tell you what kind of music your church should be using. People living in a large urban area may have different musical tastes than those living in the suburbs, a rural area, or even the Bible Belt. Every church must choose the style of music that best suits its mission and reflects the mainstream musical tastes of its constituency.

I can't tell you what intergenerational worship sounds like, but I can tell you what it looks like: it's a younger look with an older presence. That older presence may be a worship leader, a few band members, or your pastor, but the majority of those on the platform should be younger—in their twenties and thirties —not older. At Harvest Bible Chapel where I serve as pastor of worship, I'm an older presence behind the scenes, as is our pastor, but worship is led predominantly by godly men and women in their twenties and thirties. I believe that's one of the reasons we have a healthy representation of young adults at every service.

In an effort to "get younger," I've seen some churches do the opposite of what I'm advocating—they maintain an older look with a younger presence. Boomers, for example, dominate the worship team. If there are any twenty-year-olds, they're usually stuck in the back where they're hardly seen. The musical style is also geared toward Boomers. Unfortunately, this approach does nothing to attract more twenty-year-olds. It actually repels them, sending a clear message that young adults are not allowed a major role in leading worship.

Some older folks might get nervous when I talk about putting more twenty- and thirty-year-olds on the platform. They're afraid that those young adults are going to crank their guitar amps up to "11" and rock out. Pastors may be afraid of scaring away the Boomers and Builders who are the church's main financial supporters. However, every time I've reminded young worship leaders that they need to connect with the fifty-year-old businessman as well as those their own age, I've been pleasantly surprised by how much they "get it." Their penchant for authentic community causes them to be naturally inclusive in their thinking.

Why Is It Slanted toward the Young?

If you sense that the vision I'm proposing for intergenerational worship accommodates the young, you're correct. The reason for that is very practical: they're the most difficult age group to reach. They demand more prayer, effort, and intentionality. Since today's church is losing the battle in the twentysomething age demographic, we need to be more aggressive and strategic in our approach. The next generation represents the future of the church.

The Bible clearly stipulates that it is the responsibility of older believers to teach younger ones about the Lord. We are to "tell the next generation that this is God, our God forever and ever. He will guide us forever" (Psalm 48:13–14). Psalm 78 paints a vivid picture of the old imparting spiritual truth to the young:

> I will open my mouth in a parable; I will utter dark sayings from of old, things that we have heard and known, that our fathers have told us. We will not hide them from their children, but tell to the coming generation the glorious deeds of the LORD, and his might, and the wonders that he has done. He established a testimony in Jacob and appointed a law in Israel, which he commanded our fathers to teach to their children, that the next generations might know them, the children yet unborn, and arise and tell them to their children.
>
> PSALM 78:2–6

Music can be an effective tool for reaching today's young people. Psalm 89:1 says, "I will sing of the steadfast love of the LORD, forever; with my mouth I will make known your faithfulness to all generations." Bear in mind, if we're going to "sing of the steadfast love of the Lord" to twenty-year-olds, we'd better use music to which they can relate. They are a music-savvy generation. If all you give young adults is a steady stream of old songs and outdated musical styles, they'll conclude that your message, like your music, is out of touch.

It is our responsibility to teach the next generation about worship. Psalm 102:18 announces, "Let this be recorded for a generation to come, so that a people yet to be created may praise the LORD." The biggest compliment that the younger generations could pay us oldsters is found in Psalm 44:1: "O God, we have heard with our ears, our fathers have told us, what deeds you performed in their days, in the days of old." Let's take seriously our responsibility for the spiritual welfare of the next generation and cultivate in them a passion for worship.

It's Time for Us Boomers to Move Over, but Not Out

One time, after hearing me teach on intergenerational worship, a Boomer-aged woman who sang on the worship team at her church came up to me and said, "So I guess this is it; I'm done. I'm all washed up." Somehow she took me to mean that everyone over fifty years old should be put out to pasture. That's not what I'm suggesting. It's time for us Boomers to move over and share the spotlight. That doesn't mean that we must ride off into the sunset never to be heard from again.

When it comes to ministry, none of us ever retires. We serve until the day we die. In Numbers 8:25, for example, we are told that the Levites were to stop working at age fifty, but that didn't mean that they stopped ministering. Verse 26 continues, "They may assist their brothers in performing their duties at the Tent of Meeting, but they themselves must not do the work" (NIV). So even though the older Levites were exempt from heavy lifting, they still hung around and were available to help, mentor, and encourage the younger generation.

One of the highlights of my present season of life is that I have the privilege of mentoring young worship leaders. When I was their age, I distinctly remember wishing I had an older man in my life to whom I could turn for advice — someone experienced in worship ministry who could walk me through the difficulties and challenges. In the first-century church, it was common for older believers to train and encourage younger ones (see Titus 2:4–8). So if you're a Boomer, be open to mentoring young adults at your church. If my experience is any indication, it could turn out to be one of the most rewarding experiences of your life.

Heaven's Defense against Consumerism

In the two previous chapters, we discussed the negative effects of narcissism and complacency on corporate worship. However, the greatest threat to vibrant worship today is consumerism. We live in a materialistic, consumer-driven society, constantly bombarded by ads imploring us to buy this or get that because it'll make us look sexier and feel younger. If you want to be cool, you must purchase the right jeans, the latest techno toys, and the sleekest luxury car. You simply won't be happy unless you accumulate more stuff. Consumerism produces a sense of entitlement. We're not only led to believe that we can have whatever we want whenever we want it but that we *deserve* it. Advertisers insist that you not only "have it your way" but that "you deserve a break today."

Unfortunately, religious consumerism has infiltrated today's church. Too often we go to church to get, instead of give, something. This consumption mentality reduces the church to being merely a vendor of religious goods and services. For example, after a service, we typically ask each other, "How did you like the sermon?" like we're rating a new movie. We ask, "Did you enjoy the worship?" as if the purpose of the service is to entertain and hold our attention. Perhaps more pertinent questions would be, "Did you allow the Word of God to speak into your life today?" Or, "Did you offer yourself fully to the presence of God?" Or, "Did you give God your best worship this morning?"

Buyer Beware

It's completely reasonable to choose a church based on how well it ministers to you and your family. It's important to find a church that preaches God's Word and helps you grow spiritually. But beware of a consumerist disposition that expects the church to cater to your personal tastes and meet all your heartfelt needs. What you think you need may not be what God knows you need. I have a friend who explained her decision to attend a conservative Bible-preaching church by saying, "I wanted a church that would speak to me differently than how I speak to myself." She said that, if left to her own devices, she would choose a church that preached positive thinking and self-love every week instead of the full counsel of God's Word.

Beware of a sense of entitlement that causes you to think, no matter how subtly, that the church owes you something because of your dedicated service, long-term membership, or generous giving. In our opening scenario, Morgan felt entitled to hear the pipe organ because of all the time and money he gave to the church. His selfishness contributed to the committee's ineffectiveness.

I know a man who left his church because he felt the pastor didn't call on him often enough. "After all I've given to this church," he pouted, "I deserve at least a phone call every week from the senior pastor." Truth is, we serve God, not the pastor.

We are to give our tithes and offerings to the Lord's work with no strings attached.

Those with a nagging sense of entitlement tend to be overly negative, demanding, and critical of the church and its leaders. They also resist change or new ideas. Decisions that don't go their way are taken as personal insults. If you're threatened by changes at church or chronically indignant toward new ideas, it's time to ask whether your own personal agenda is clouding objectivity.

Church Is a Privilege

Consumerism and self-entitlement reflect attitudes that contradict the teachings of Christ. If anyone were entitled to royal privileges, it would have been the Son of God. Yet, he "did not count equality with God a thing to be grasped, but made himself nothing, taking the form of a servant" (Philippians 2:6–7). Jesus loves the church and "gave himself up for her" (Ephesians 5:25). He "came not to be served but to serve" (Mark 10:45). It is simply unbecoming for a Christ follower to demand that the church indulge every whim and fancy. No church is perfect, and yours may even have serious problems, but we are called to love the church as Christ loves it and faithfully serve the Lord through the ministry of a local church.

Psalm 84 depicts a man who loves and appreciates God's house. He enthusiastically states, "For a day in your courts is better than a thousand elsewhere. I would rather be a doorkeeper in the house of my God than dwell in the tents of wickedness" (Psalm 84:10). The psalmist doesn't come across as if the church owes him something. Even if it means being an obscure lowly doorman, he's happy to be in the company of fellow worshipers.

Likewise, David's words in Psalm 65:4 are a far cry from the negative attitudes found in many modern churchgoers. He said, "We shall be satisfied with the goodness of your house, the holiness of your temple!" Instead of bad-mouthing the church or nit-picking what he doesn't like about the service, David savors the privilege of worshiping in the house of God.

Taking a Stand against Consumerism

I served on the staff of Willow Creek Community church for many years. Amid all that's been written about Willow's innovations, one thing that's often overlooked was Willow's uncanny ability to convince its core of otherwise selfish suburbanites that church is not a country club. Weekend "seeker services" featured music, drama, video, and sermons geared toward non-Christians. Mid-week "New Community" services favored worship and biblical teaching aimed at building up believers. On Sundays, we would sit through the service praying for unsaved friends or neighbors we had invited, filtering every aspect of the service through their eyes. It never occurred to any of us to demand that the service indulge our personal tastes and preferences. After all, the service

TAKEAWAY #7:

Set Aside Personal Preferences

In order for the generations to worship peaceably alongside each other (as in heaven), we all need to set aside our personal preferences, especially, as we shall see, in regard to musical styles. Even if your church conducts age-segregated services and never embraces intergenerational worship, setting aside personal preferences is a universal principle that will free you up to worship God on his terms, not yours.

was not for us; it was for unbelievers. The Willow philosophy of ministry has its strengths and weaknesses, but I will never forget the valuable lesson I learned during my years there: that church is not just for me; there are plenty of others in the room as well. That was, and still is today, a countercultural idea. But since I've already seen it happen once in my lifetime, I hold out hope that today's church can also take a stand against consumerism.

Heroic Deference

I once heard someone say that life in the body of Christ calls for "heroic deference," which is defined as a selfless, courteous regard for the needs of others. As 1 Corinthians 10:24 exhorts, "Let no one seek his own good, but the good of his neighbor." To the church at Philippi, Paul wrote, "Let each of you look not only to his own interests, but also to the interests of others" (Philippians 2:4). Can you imagine a church where everyone arrived on Sunday morning without a personal agenda? That was the trademark of the first-century church: "Now the full number of those who believed were of one heart and soul, and no one said that any of the things that belonged to him was his own, but they had everything in common" (Acts 4:32). When it comes to issues of Christian doctrine, we are to conform to biblical theology. When it comes to matters of personal taste, we are to demonstrate deference. In all things, we are to exhibit love.

Corporate worship is an ideal opportunity to practice heroic deference. Referring once again to our opening scenario, in spite of Christina's insistence that committee members put the needs of the congregation first, each of them tried to foist their musical preferences on others. After encouraging us to minister to each other in psalms, hymns, and spiritual songs, Paul adds that we should do so "submitting to one another out of reverence for

Christ" (Ephesians 5:21). Setting aside your personal preferences in music for the greater good of the church is an act of submission and a sign of Christian character. It is unrealistic for the church to play your "Personal Worship Mix" every week.

Sing Old *and* New Songs

Practicing heroic deference means that we make every effort to sing praise songs from outside our particular age group. In heaven, we will sing old songs, like the song of Moses described in Revelation 15:3–4. But we will also sing new songs (Revelation 5:9; 14:3). The book of Psalms is a collection of ancient songs that still minister to us today. However, that same book instructs us over and over to sing to the Lord a "new song" (Psalm 33:3; 40:3; 96:1; 98:1; 144:9; 149:1). Most experts believe that the "spiritual songs" Paul instructs us to sing in Ephesians 5:19 are actually new original compositions.[53]

As you grow older, be open to singing new praise music, especially that of the next generation. Go a step further and encourage young musicians in your church to write and play original music that captures their generation's passion for God. Romans 15:1 teaches that heroic deference begins with those of us who are older in the faith: "We who are strong have an obligation to bear with the failings of the weak, and not to please ourselves." Of all people, veteran Christians should be giving, patient, and tolerant, not selfish and demanding.

If you're young, show respect for the worship music of previous generations and be open to singing some of those old tunes. Deuteronomy 32:7 invites young people to "remember the days of old; consider the years of many generations; ask your father, and he will show you, your elders, and they will tell you." Don't let the date of a song prevent you from worshiping.

Jesus said, "Therefore every scribe who has been trained for the kingdom of heaven is like a master of a house, who brings out of his treasure what is new and what is old" (Matthew 13:52). If you want to experience worship on earth as it is in heaven, be open to singing both old and new worship music.

No More Worship Wars

If we all practiced heroic deference, there would be no more nasty disputes over musical styles like the "worship wars" that have divided many a church. We've all seen blatant examples of intolerance, like the disgruntled parishioner who sits through the service with arms folded across the chest, stubbornly refusing to sing. Or the church veteran who's offended by the new "ungodly" music and threatens to leave or quit tithing. Or the young person who mocks the older generation's music for being "unspiritual" or "inauthentic." In spite of these strong opinions, the Bible does not endorse one style of music over another; no type of music is more holy than the others.

Historically, every new idea related to musical worship was always greeted at first by staunch opposition. Writing about the introduction of the organ in the seventh century, historian Philip Schaff points out:

> The attitude of the churches towards the organ varies.... The Greek church disapproves the use of organs. The Latin church introduced it pretty generally, but not without the protest of eminent men, so that even in the Council of Trent a motion was made, though not carried, to prohibit the organ at least in the mass. The Lutheran church retained it, the Calvinistic churches rejected it, especially in Switzerland and Scotland.[54]

The first time part-singing was introduced, it caused an uproar because the prevailing mindset insisted that everyone should sing in unison. Even the earliest hymns, when first unveiled, were rejected by those who insisted that the psalms were the only legitimate songs for worship. So even the most venerated staples of church music were once controversial innovations.

In 1 Corinthians 1:10, Paul puts out an urgent plea for unity: "I appeal to you, brothers, by the name of our Lord Jesus Christ, that all of you agree, and that there be no divisions among you, but that you be united in the same mind and the same judgment." It would be a shame for any church to stand before God someday and say, "Sorry, Lord. We weren't able to come together in unity because we were too busy bickering about how to worship you."

Serious worshipers, therefore, steer clear of any and all worship wars. Romans 14:19 encourages us to "pursue what makes for peace and for mutual upbuilding." So don't get pulled into any skirmishes over worship styles. They do nothing but sow strife and disunity.

At this point I can't resist a little twist on a war protest song from the turbulent '60s. Think of it as a protest against worship wars:

> *Worship wars, huh, yeah.*
> *What are they good for?*
> *Absolutely nothing.*
> *Uh-huh.*
> *Worship wars, huh, yeah.*
> *What are they good for?*
> *Absolutely nothing.*
> *Say it again, y'all.*[55]

What Would You Give?

I'm sure you know people who don't know Christ, and I trust you're praying for them regularly. May I ask how many of those on your prayer list are young adults—unsaved sons, daughters, nephews, nieces, or neighborhood kids? Do you know any young loved ones who have turned their backs on God, hooked up with the wrong crowd, and shipwrecked their lives? Do you have a prodigal son or daughter who's gone astray, rejecting not only God but friends and family as well? What would you do to bring that lost one to faith? Chances are you would do absolutely *anything* for that young one to come to Christ. Therefore, if we're all willing to do *anything* to reach young people, is it too much to ask that we set aside our personal preferences in music in order to win the next generation for Christ? Seems like a small price to pay in seeking the eternal salvation of our young friends and loved ones.

Ponder and Apply

1 What do you think about the vision for intergenerational worship that's described in this chapter?

2 Do you agree that a consumerist mentality has infiltrated the church today? Why or why not?

3 Is there a specific personal preference you need to set aside in order to fully engage in worship at your church? If so, what is it?

4 Do you have any other ideas on how to promote unity among the generations at your church? If so, what are they?

5 Is there any way churches can avoid worship wars? If so, how?

FOR PASTORS AND WORSHIP LEADERS

If you're interested in pursuing intergenerational worship at your church, I suggest you start by inviting some twenty-year-olds to participate in service planning meetings. Listen to their ideas and incorporate as many as possible. Involve as many young adults in services as you can.

It might also prove helpful to get some old church members together with a group of young adults to dialogue about worship. Make it low-key and informal; schedule the get-together around a meal, coffee, or dessert. Stay away from controversy at the outset. Instead, ask questions like:

- What are your favorite worship songs and why?
- What was the most meaningful or memorable worship experience you've ever had?
- What helps facilitate worship for you?

Encourage young and old to talk about what worship means to them. Share stories across the age spectrum of your favorite worship experiences. As Psalm 79:13 says, "From generation to generation we will recount your praise." Getting different generations to listen to each other as we talk about the Lord could go a long way in building bridges among us.

CHAPTER 8

Welcome Every Tribe and Nation
Embrace Diversity

Terry got home from church late last night. After choir rehearsal, he ran back to his office in the church basement to drop off his music, thinking his night was over. Far from it. Taped to Terry's door was a note from his pastor: "See me before you leave tonight."

As Terry made his way to the pastor's office, his mind was racing: *Was there another complaint about the music? Was it too loud? Did the pastor not like last Sunday's choir selections?* Terry could see the light on in the pastor's study. He tapped lightly on the door.

"Come in," Pastor Pete said. His desk was littered with books, papers, and a towering stack of mail. "Have a seat, Terry." The pastor looked pained and troubled.

"You have a problem," he blurted out as Terry sat down. Pastor Pete never was one to beat around the bush. "You have a serious problem," he added, nodding his head.

Terry waited, holding his breath.

Pastor Pete looked him straight in the eye and all he said was, "Rodney."

Oh, Rodney, Terry thought. *I should have known.*

Rodney and his wife, Linda, started attending the church three months ago. They made quite a first impression, pulling up to the front door in a pair of vintage Harley Davidson motorcycles. His was black, hers was pink. They stepped slowly off their bikes, studied the building for a minute, and then walked into the sanctuary just as the sermon was starting. Pastor Pete stopped mid-sentence, and everyone turned around to look. There in the back stood Rodney and Linda in all their tattooed, black-leathered, and silver-chained glory. Well into his middle age, Rodney sported a gray beard, wore a red-white-and-blue headband, and had a large gold earring in one ear and several little ones in the other. Linda had flamingo-colored hair and a silver nose ring. With all eyes trained to the back of the room, Rodney grinned and shouted, "Hello, everyone! My name is Rodney, and this here is my wife, Linda. We just wanted to check out what y'all do here on Sunday morning." A couple ushers jumped to their feet, greeted the newcomers, shook their hands, offered bulletins, and seated them near the door.

That was the day Rodney's and Linda's lives were changed forever. Toward the end of the sermon, Pastor Pete invited anyone wanting to make a decision to follow Christ to come forward for prayer. Rodney and Linda were the first ones out of their seats, tears streaming down their faces. A month later, they were baptized and enrolled in a new believers class. They even joined the choir, where Rodney could be seen in the front row every week sporting his trademark headband. That headband was the reason Terry was called on the carpet.

"The headband's gotta go," Pastor Pete said. "I'm getting complaints all the time about it."

"I know." Terry sighed. "I don't know what else to do. I've talked to the choir about not being a distraction. We've warned everyone not to stick out and not to wear anything that calls attention to oneself. It's part of the covenant we all sign."

"You need to be more direct," Pastor Pete insisted. "Have you asked him personally not to wear the headband when he's up front?"

"Well, no, not exactly," Terry admitted. "I've joked about it. I think he knows I don't care for it, but I've never really come out and told him not to wear it."

"You need to tell him to take off the headband or he's out of the choir."

There was an awkward pause. "I don't know if I can do that, Pastor," Terry replied. Another awkward pause. "I'm sorry, but I'm struggling with this."

"Look, I know it's difficult," Pete said. "We all love Rodney and Linda. We're all thrilled at what God's doing in their lives. The headband is not a big problem for me personally. But some people are put off. They think Rodney's being disrespectful. For his own good, he needs to lose the headband. And you need to confront him on it before Sunday."

Terry sighed. "I'll see what I can do."

Discussion Questions

1 Do you agree with Pastor Pete's request for Rodney to remove his headband? Why, or why not?

2 What advice do you have for those in the congregation who are distracted by Rodney's headband?

3 What would you do if you were in Terry's shoes?

4 What advice do you have for Rodney about wearing his headband in the choir?

5 Are there any Scriptures you could bring to bear on this issue?

Heavenly Worship Is Multiethnic

In eternity, people of all races, from different cultures, will stand together as one and worship our great God. John describes this beautiful tapestry of multiethnic worship in Revelation 7:9–10:

> After this I looked, and behold, a great multitude that no one could number, from every nation, from all tribes and peoples and languages, standing before the throne and before the Lamb, clothed in white robes, with palm branches in their hands, and crying out with a loud voice, "Salvation belongs to our God who sits on the throne, and to the Lamb!"

Earlier John had observed the heavenly host bowing down before the Lamb of God, who has ransomed a multiethnic multitude "from every tribe and language and people and nation" and "made them a kingdom and priests to our God" (Revelation 5:9–10). The heavenly choir isn't divided into separate ethnic groups. John witnesses a glorious mix of people—a blur and blend of color and custom—standing side by side worshiping God.

A Growing Trend

According to the *Washington Post*, the United States Census Bureau projects that by the year 2042, minorities, who currently comprise a third of the population, will become the nation's majority. By the middle of this century, there will be no single majority racial or ethnic group in the United States. Specifically, the Hispanic population will triple by 2050, "growing from about one in six residents to one in three. The black and Asian populations are each expected to increase about 60 percent, with the black share rising from 14 to 15 percent by 2050 and the Asian share jumping from 5 to 9 percent.... By contrast, the non-Hispanic, single-race white population is expected to grow by less than 2 percent, reducing its share of the overall population from 66 to 46 percent."[56] Like much of Europe and other parts of the world, the United States is fast becoming a blended, multicultural society.

Today's Increasingly Multiethnic Congregation

Today, more and more churches reflect this growing trend toward greater ethnic diversity. As local churches witness an influx of minorities, astute leaders are striving to be more inclusive in their approach. For example, many churches are trying to include minorities on staff, in leadership roles, and on the platform. Others might feature a verse of a song or an entire tune in Spanish. Scripture may be read in multiple languages. In some cases, headsets are made available for sermon translation. Music from Africa, South America, or the Caribbean may be heard. The multiethnic church is the wave of the future. Some predict it will emerge as the dominant strategy for church growth during the twenty-first century.

More "Us" Than We Realize

I know a worship leader who serves at a suburban church in the Midwest. His congregation is predominantly white, but, like the community, is growing in diversity. My friend recently invited a team from a nearby African American church to lead worship. The musicians were exceptionally talented. Their love for the Lord was infectious. They introduced gospel songs the congregation had never heard before and moved to the beat of the music with more freedom than the church was used to seeing on their platform — some might even describe it as dancing. In spite of their different approach, the guest worship leaders were warmly received and enthusiastically applauded, especially among the African Americans in attendance, most of whom stood and clapped throughout the worship set.

Afterward, describing the service to me, my friend referred to the guest worship leaders and said, "At first, I wasn't sure if their style was really 'us.' But given the growing number of African Americans we have in our congregation, it's obvious that we are no longer a homogeneous church. I guess the music was more 'us' than I realized."

In multiethnic churches, there is just one big "us"—the family of God, the bride of Christ, the church.

Multiethnic Worship throughout Scripture

Multicultural worship is a vital issue not because it's the latest trend or because "the neighborhood is changing," but because it is scriptural. God's vision for multiethnic worship echoes throughout the Bible. The psalms paint a vivid picture of diverse nationalities coming together to worship. "All the nations you have made shall come and worship before you, O Lord, and shall glorify your name" (Psalm 86:9). David pictures himself amidst the worldwide family of God when he writes, "I will give thanks to you, O Lord, among the peoples; I will sing praises to you among the nations" (Psalm 57:9). Psalm 106:47 reads, "Save us, O LORD our God, and gather us from among the nations, that we may give thanks to your holy name and glory in your praise." Multiethnic worship is not some trendy new idea, nor is it reserved exclusively for heaven; it is the way God has always intended worship to be.

The Cause of Christ

Jesus brought various culture groups together by preaching a message of unconditional love and brotherhood. The Good Samaritan is the story of someone from a minority culture reaching across the racial divide to help another in need. Jesus' invitation to "worship the Father in spirit and truth" was first spoken to a Samaritan woman (John 4:23; see vv. 7 – 30), who, being a Samaritan, a woman, and a divorcée five times over, faced discrimination her whole life.

Jesus proclaimed himself the Good Shepherd, who laid down his life for his sheep. "And I have other sheep that are not of this fold," he said, referring to the Gentiles. "I must bring them also, and they will listen to my voice. So there will be one flock, one shepherd" (John 10:14 – 16). Jesus' clear intention is not only to ransom people from every nation but to unite us under the banner of his love.

When he drove the greedy salesmen out of the temple and overturned the tables of the money changers, Jesus cried out, "Is it not written, 'My house shall be called a house of prayer *for all the nations*'?" (Mark 11:17, emphasis added). In Jesus' day, the temple had become blatantly inhospitable, especially toward Gentiles and foreigners, who were easy targets for unscrupulous merchants. Jesus not only cleansed the temple of greed but of discrimination and the injustices perpetrated against Gentiles, minorities, and foreigners.

Before ascending into heaven, Jesus told his followers, "Go therefore and make disciples of all nations, baptizing them in the name of the Father and of the Son and of the Holy Spirit" (Matthew 28:19). He instructed them (us) to be his witnesses "in Jerusalem and in all Judea and Samaria, and to the end of the earth" (Acts 1:8). These two verses are often the catalyst for foreign missions. Jesus' mandate for evangelism and discipleship is to be carried out not only abroad but also among the various ethnic groups in our own backyard.

Trademark of the Early Church

The church was born out of a cross-cultural worship experience. On the day of Pentecost, diverse nationalities came together to worship in a powerful way:

> Now there were dwelling in Jerusalem Jews, devout men from every nation under heaven. And at this sound the multitude came together, and they were bewildered, because each one was hearing them speak in his own language. And they were amazed and astonished, saying, "Are not all these who are speaking Galileans? And how is it that we hear, each of us in his own native language? . . . We hear them telling in our own tongues the mighty works of God."
>
> ACTS 2:5–8, 11

The ancient Jews were notoriously exclusive. They turned the privilege of being God's chosen people into a source of pride and prejudice. They looked down on Gentiles and wanted nothing to do with them. We can only imagine the dilemma facing first-century Christians when Peter received a vision for the church as a place where all are welcome regardless of race. Peter said, "Truly I understand that God shows no partiality, but in every nation anyone who fears him and does what is right is acceptable to him" (Acts 10:34–35). Instead of a closed system available to only a chosen few, Peter proclaimed that Christianity is open to everyone. As a result, many of the church's first converts included minorities and Gentiles. Dramatic accounts of the Samaritans (Acts 8:5–25), an Ethiopian (Acts 8:26–40), and a Roman soldier (Acts 10) coming to Christ underscore the fact that the church is for all who want to come, regardless of background or ethnicity.

Like today, the New Testament world was comprised of diverse and sometimes contentious cultures. Yet Christ brought them together—"Greek and Jew, circumcised and uncircumcised, barbarian, Scythian, slave, free" (Colossians 3:11). In Christ, people who were otherwise alienated from one another were brought together in community. "For he himself is our peace, who has made us both one and has broken down in his flesh the dividing wall of hostility" (Ephesians 2:14). With Christ as their cornerstone, churches in the first century were typically integrated, not segregated.

The First Church of Antioch

The church at Antioch, highlighted extensively throughout the book of Acts, was especially rich with ethnic diversity. A large Syrian city, Antioch was known as a bustling economic and cultural center. Its population was very diverse, comprised of mostly Greek-speaking Gentiles as well as Jews. It is significant that believers were first called "Christians" or followers of Christ at Antioch (Acts 11:26). Evidently, the rest of the city observed Jews and Gentiles getting along and loving each other, and they rightfully credited the teachings of Jesus Christ for this unlikely alliance and camaraderie.

One of the most intriguing aspects of the Antioch church was the diversity of its leadership. As Acts 13:1 reveals, "Now there were in the church at Antioch prophets and teachers, Barnabas, Simeon who was called Niger, Lucius of Cyrene, Manaen a member of the court of Herod the tetrarch, and Saul." Significantly, these leaders were from vastly diverse backgrounds. Barnabas was from Cyprus (Acts 4:36) in the Mediterranean. Simeon hailed from Niger in West Africa, Lucius from northern Africa, and Manaen from Palestine. Paul was from Tarsus, a Roman city in Asia Minor (Acts 9:11). So overseeing this multiethnic church were two men from Africa, one from the Mediterranean, one from the Middle East, and one a Jew with Roman citizenship from Asia Minor. In other words, the leadership team of this church reflected the ethnic diversity of its congregation.

It's no coincidence that the Antioch church was known for its generosity and its work with missions. Antioch was the first church to take up a collection for the victims of famine in Judea (Acts 11:27–30). The church also sent out Paul and others on at least three missionary trips abroad (Acts 13:2–14:28; 15:35–18:22; 18:22–20:3). Due to its own ethnic and economic diversity, the church in Antioch had a heart for the poor and was quick to reach out to others beyond its own walls. Take note: the local church given the most press in the book of Acts was a vibrant multiethnic congregation.

TAKEAWAY #8:
Embrace Diversity

Whether you attend an urban church that's teeming with ethnicity or live in a rural area with few minorities, church life offers plenty of opportunities to embrace diversity. That's because diversity is not just a racial issue. We are all different in myriads of ways. We are all one, but we are not all the same. If we're to live in harmony with each other and glorify the Lord as one voice (Romans 15:5–6), we all need to learn how to get along with each other in spite of our diverse ages, personalities, temperaments, political views, social standings, economic means, and educational backgrounds. Let's explore further what it means to embrace diversity, especially in the context of corporate worship.

Accept Those Different from You

The most important thing we can do to embrace diversity is to accept others, especially those who think, talk, or act differently than we do. Romans 15:7 says, "Therefore welcome one another as Christ has welcomed you, for the glory of God." Accepting others means that we welcome them with open arms, that we're patient with their shortcomings. Accepting others means that we don't vilify those with differing political views or demand that people conform to our liking but encourage them to be all God created them to be. We do this for the glory of God, which makes it another way to express worship.

The earliest conflict in the history of the church revolved around the way minorities were treated. Every day the Jerusalem church distributed food and provisions to members who were poor and needy. However, there was a group of Greek-speaking Jewish widows, known as Hellenists, who were being overlooked and neglected, probably due to the language barrier. To solve the problem, leaders appointed seven men fluent in Greek to serve the widows (Acts 6:1–6). The church didn't ignore or minimize the needs of minorities. Leaders didn't smugly insist the widows learn to speak Aramaic before helping them. The church took action to minister to minorities and let them know they were welcome.

Referring to this chapter's opening scenario, does your church have people like Rodney and Linda who are different from everyone else? People some might find unacceptable? Romans 12:10 instructs church people to "love one another with brotherly affection. Outdo one another in showing honor." When it comes to loving the folks at church, we are to go out of our way to extend grace, mercy, and love to all, including those who are difficult, different, or disagreeable. Accepting others is never an excuse to minimize sin or compromise our faith. Even when denouncing sin, we are to treat people with love, courtesy, and respect, never with disdain (Titus 3:2).

Is there anyone at church you find particularly difficult to love and accept? Is there anyone with whom you have a hard time getting along? Have you reached out to any minorities at your church, greeted them, or made them feel welcome? Ask the Lord for the strength to accept those different from you and then warmly extend the hand of fellowship to them.

Celebrate the Variety of the Spirit's Work

Embracing diversity also means that we celebrate the various ways the Holy Spirit works in the world. Hearing black gospel music, singing a song with a Latin tempo, or listening to Scripture read in another language all remind us that we are part of a global community of believers. "All the earth worships you and sings praises to you; they sing praises to your name" (Psalm 66:4). Multiethnic worship also assures us that God is at work, not only in our little corner of the world but also across the entire planet. "All the ends of the earth shall remember and turn to the Lord, and all the families of the nations shall worship before you" (Psalm 22:27).

Many Different Ways to Worship

The Bible teaches that the Holy Spirit accomplishes the work of God in a variety of ways. First Corinthians 12:4–6 reveals that "there are varieties of gifts, but the same Spirit; and there are varieties of service, but the same Lord; and there are varieties of activities, but it is the same God who empowers them all in everyone." In the same way, there is a wide variety of worship styles throughout Christendom. From one culture to the next, from one denomination to the next, from one local church to the next, there are numerous customs and traditions associated with worship, and that is something to be celebrated. No one style of worship could encompass all the possible ways there are to praise God. No one style of worship is adequate in and of itself to fully express all there is to say about a God who is infinite and eternal. "Who can utter the mighty deeds of the LORD, or declare all his praise?" (Psalm 106:2).

Don't latch on to one style of music as the "right way" or the only way to worship. Don't be quick to criticize how others worship or condemn their tastes in music. Engage with music from another culture or Christian tradition as best you can. Follow the example of David who said, "I will give thanks to you, O LORD, among the peoples; I will sing praises to you among the nations" (Psalm 108:3). Join in and celebrate all the various ways Christians express worship to the Lord!

In Defense of Christian Rap (and Other Contemporary Styles)

Recently at my church, we featured a Christian "rap" song performed by a godly young African American man named Johnnie. Our worship leader set up the song by introducing Johnnie as a friend, a brother in Christ, and an active member of our church who may sing a different musical language but still very much loves and worships the Lord. It was important to us that our people know that Johnnie is part of our fellowship. He wasn't a "ringer" we brought in for the sake of diversity. We were merely stewarding the gifts God has placed in our body. Our pastor was fully supportive[57] and most of the feedback we received was overwhelmingly positive. However, I received emails from a few people who were offended by the fact that we used a rap song in church. One man in particular threatened to leave the church because of it.

Disagreement over the use of the arts in church is nothing new. In my lifetime alone, churches have faced controversy over rock music, jazz, blues, drums, electric guitar, and saxophones as well as dance, drama, and video, which, ironically, are all commonplace in churches today but originally struggled for acceptance. So how are we to respond to new innovations in worship? How should we react to changes in the church service? I'd like to offer some simple guidelines for such discussion. I'll use Christian rap as an example, but the following principles can be applied to other innovations in worship as well.

1. *Consider the words.* When evaluating whether a song is appropriate for church, look first at the lyrics. Do they glorify God? Are they true? Do they espouse sound doctrine? Similarly, if it's an art form that's in question, consider its message. The congregation should never be asked to sing or listen to words that violate biblical truth. People may not like a type of music because it's not their "cup of tea," but they should never be able to criticize the theological integrity of the lyrics. In that regard, our leadership went over the songs Johnnie sang with a fine-tooth comb, as we do with all our music, and signed off on their content.

2. *Don't misjudge an artist's motives.* It grieves me when a musician is vilified for trying to introduce innovation into worship. While it's true that some Christian artists have massive egos, the majority of the ones I know are serious about serving the Lord and living for him. You might not care for a certain worship leader's brand of music, but don't

be so quick to judge his or her motives. Believe the best until evidence proves otherwise (1 Corinthians 13:7).

In our example, Johnnie is the real deal. Even if you don't like rap music, you can't deny that he's sold out to Jesus Christ. Furthermore, the words to Johnnie's songs are bold and zealous, yet his humility and genuine faith come through loud and clear as he sings.

3. *Avoid generalizations, stereotypes, and assumptions.* Shortly after Johnnie sang, I received an email from a man who went on a tirade against rap music, similar to the ones I used to hear when I was in my twenties about the evils of rock music in church. Throughout the email, several assumptions and generalizations were made, the most outrageous being that no one listens to rap music anymore. When discussing music in worship, avoid making sweeping statements. If you doubt whether rap music fits the demographic of your church, you need to know that rap has been around for a couple decades now and is more popular than ever. No longer confined to one ethnic subculture, rap has become mainstream. In many churches, there may be more fans of rap music than most realize. Furthermore, many men, who are turned off by the flowery language of some of today's worship music, are drawn to Christian rap because of its bold testimony and call to action. These days, fans of Christian rap far outnumber its detractors.

4. *Music is neither right nor wrong.* You may be okay with Christian rap, but don't think it's appropriate for church. Be careful about drawing such conclusions. After all, the Bible offers plenty of examples of what kind of words are fit for worship, but offers no clue as to what type of music should be used. There is a great deal of latitude when it comes to musical styles in worship. This is where

it gets tricky; what one church decides is right for them, another may deem as totally inappropriate, offensive, even immoral. However, music, without the words, is amoral. The particular arrangement of musical notes into melody, harmony, and rhythm is neither right nor wrong—they're just notes. So avoid making musical style, or any other matter of preference, a moral issue. It would be truer to say that a particular style of music doesn't fit your tradition than to say that it's inappropriate for church.

5. *Negative associations with music can be reversed.* The two Bible verses most often quoted in opposition to Christian rap and other contemporary styles are Philippians 4:8 ("whatever is pure ... think about these things") and 1 Thessalonians 5:22 (avoid even the appearance of evil). However, aside from the lyrics, which should always be God-honoring, the question of whether the music is impure or gives the impression of evil is subjective. Most often, it's the negative associations we bring to music that prompt us to dismiss it as wrong or immoral.

The controversy around rap music, and other styles, centers most often upon its association with the world. In this case, rap music has an extremely dubious association with violence, murder, and rape, all of which are undeniably deplorable. As I was growing up, rock music in church drew equally strong reproach because of its association with sex, drugs, and rebellion. I don't want to minimize negative associations with music, but we shouldn't throw out the rich sounds of rap because of the offensive words attached to it by some. Besides, negative associations may be strong for some people but not exist at all for others.

I am not naïve about what secular rap music stands for, and I certainly don't endorse the lifestyle for which some rap artists are known. However, those of us who support Christian rap are thrilled that a musical genre once dominated by Satan has been recovered for Jesus. Music that used to glorify evil is now used to glorify God. An art form that used to be associated with violence is now aligned with the Prince of Peace. And isn't that what Christ wants to do in the world, in our communities, and in our lives —take that which was controlled by sin and bring it into submission to the Holy Spirit? Jesus desires that we "turn from darkness to light and from the power of Satan to God" (Acts 26:18). "The reason the Son of God appeared was to destroy the works of the devil" (1 John 3:8). God is in the business of defeating evil and making all things new (2 Corinthians 5:17; Revelation 21:5).

Negative associations may be hard to shake, and I'm not asking you to suddenly love rap music. But instead of condemning it, I encourage you to celebrate the fact that God is using Christian rap to bring thousands of people to Christ and that guys like Johnnie, who used to sing about death and Satan, are now singing about new life in Christ.

Be Willing to Learn from Others

Psalm 117:1 calls the nations to worship: "Praise the LORD, all nations! Extol him, all peoples!" Psalm 67:4 adds, "Let the nations be glad and sing for joy." However, not every nation praises God the same way or with the same kind of music. Every culture puts its own unique stamp on worship. Therefore, we can learn a great deal about how to worship from Christians outside our own tradition or ethnic group. In my travels, I've had the privilege of observing some of the many different ways Christians worship. I'd like to briefly highlight three such examples. I don't consider myself an expert in these particular styles of worship or their cultures, but my experiences with each have been deeply meaningful and have taught me much about worship.

Learning from Our Brothers and Sisters of African Descent

If you've ever attended a black church, you undoubtedly noticed that African American worship often generates a great deal of energy. Although denominations differ in style, worship in many black churches is usually loud and celebratory with a lot of singing, clapping, and dancing. It is also highly interactive. Few sit still; almost everyone participates. Generally, worship in the African tradition is highly experiential; emotion is welcomed and encouraged. African Americans come to church not only to learn something but also to experience God's Spirit moving actively during the service. In a conversation with my friend Dr. Debby Mitchell, she told me:

> Much of the African American church experience evolved from the slave church. It was the only time/place where there was some degree of freedom. The people's faith was deeply grounded in their belief that God would deliver them from their oppression. Openness to the supernatural was necessary to literally survive from one week to the other.

Indeed, African worship encourages freedom of expression, especially when it comes to music. Songs, for example, are rarely sung or played the same way every time. Melodies are altered, chords substituted, and lines improvised "as the Spirit leads." Much of the music is learned by ear. If there is any written sheet music, it's usually just lyrics and chords. Vocal parts are fluid and flexible, changing from one week to the next. Thus, individual expression is encouraged. People are invited to praise God in their own unique way. As a result, the music sounds free and spontaneous.

Author Brenda Aghaowa is quick to point out that black worship is highly relational:

Frequent visitors to black worship will know of its relational character. Worshipers might be instructed to ask the names of those sitting next to them, to shake hands with people around them or to turn to their neighbors and say, "God bless you" or "I don't know what *you* came to do, but *I* came to praise the Lord." Or they might be instructed to leave their seats for a brief period of time and go around the sanctuary to hug and greet as many people as they can. Often, for the benediction, worshipers may be asked to join hands, even across aisles, for the final doxology. All will sway together rhythmically in time to the music as they sing a gospel version of "Praise God from Whom All Blessings Flow." The clasped hands are lifted to the ceiling as the final Amen of a threefold "Amen" concludes the doxology.[58]

The sermon in most black churches is more like a dialogue than a lecture, like preaching rather than teaching. Multicultural church expert David A. Anderson notes the difference:

> Paul told Timothy to preach and teach the Word. I admit that the following statement is a huge generalization, but I have noticed that white churches focus on "teaching the Word" and black churches focus on "preaching the Word." Good multicultural churches do both.
>
> Teaching focuses on information; preaching focuses on inspiration.... We have found that whites, generally speaking, like information. If they don't feel like they've learned something, then church, while it may have been a nice experience, wasn't the best way to spend their time. Blacks, on the other hand, generally speaking, prefer inspiration. If they don't feel like they've been motivated to act or respond, then the message, while it may have been good, was not moving. My comments must be taken as generalizations because there are many blacks who want information and

whites who want inspiration. But I think the trends are broadly true.[59]

Because of the inspirational/motivational preaching and the fact that "call and response" is rooted in African culture, African American churchgoers are famous for calling out responses during the sermon. Spontaneous phrases like "Amen!" or "Preach it!" or "You tell 'em!" often punctuate the preaching.

There is much to be gleaned from worship born out of the African culture. Indeed, worship that is energetic, celebratory, free, spontaneous, relational, and inspirational would certainly be a welcome addition to anyone's private and/or corporate worship experience.

Learning from Our Brothers and Sisters of Hispanic Descent

Hispanic culture is known for its strong sense of "fiesta," or celebration. Hispanics love to be together and have a good time. By the same token, a Hispanic church service is characteristically upbeat with a healthy dose of fun, joy, and laughter. There is also a lot of physical activity, including rhythmical music, dancing, and clapping. Hispanic worship is highly interactive. It is not a performance put on by professionals. Everyone is invited to join in. The choir doesn't necessarily exist to perform but to encourage the congregation to sing.

Hispanic worship is also very passionate and emotive. Holy Week services, for instance, may include graphic reenactments of Christ's suffering and death, complete with an actor carrying a large wooden cross through the church and eventually suspended on it for the crucifixion scene.

There's a feeling of spontaneity to Hispanic worship that resists any hint of being scripted or programmed. Author Justo Gonzalez explains further:

First of all, because worship is a fiesta rather than a performance, it may be planned, but not rehearsed. Oftentimes Hispanic worship seems chaotic. Indeed, there are some Hispanic pastors and other leaders who are remiss in that they do not even plan the celebration, but simply let it happen. But in most cases the difference between our worship and that of the dominant culture is that we think in terms of planning a party rather than rehearsing a performance. Certainly choirs and bands rehearse; but the service, as such, is never rehearsed. We plan, as one does for a fiesta, in order to make sure that necessary arrangements have been made. In the case of a fiesta, one arranges for enough food and chairs, for a mariachi or some other kind of music, and for parking. But one cannot actually plan all the details, as one does in a performance, because the success of the fiesta depends on the attitude and participation of those present, not just of the performers. Likewise, in worship the celebration is the people's fiesta, and therefore the pastor and other worship leaders can plan only up to a point, leaving the rest to the celebrants themselves — and, as many Hispanics would stress, to the guidance of the Holy Spirit.[60]

Finally, going to church is a family activity. From aging grandparents to newborns, all attend together. However, this spirit of solidarity goes beyond one's immediate family to also include the church family. Hispanics have what author Juana Bordas describes as a strong sense of "we." She adds that "we cultures" have a strong sense of belonging and sticking together, are impeccably inclusive, and put benefiting the whole before the individual. In "we cultures," the "I" exists only in relationship to others, not as a separate entity.[61] This strong sense of unity explains why Hispanics typically hug and kiss upon arriving as well as leaving church and why they linger long after the service is over to fellowship.

As with African worship, there is much we can learn from our Hispanic brothers and sisters about praising the Lord. We could all certainly be more joyful, celebratory, passionate, spontaneous, and unified in our worship.

Learning from the Brothers at Taizé

Every year, more than 100,000 young people from all over the world embark on a spiritual pilgrimage to a tiny village in the south of France called Taizé, which is home to an ecumenical monastic order devoted to prayer, peace, and justice. I visited Taizé a few years ago, and their approach has greatly influenced the way I lead worship for the Transforming Center, the retreat ministry alluded to earlier for pastors and lay leaders. A number of Taizé songs have become favorites at our retreats.

At Taizé, three times a day, at set hours, church bells ring, and everyone drops whatever they're doing and heads to the chapel for prayer. Upon entering, everyone grabs a flimsy little staple-bound songbook. This was my first clue that the brothers of Taizé are a simple, no-frills community. By the same token, worship at Taizé is refreshingly low-tech. There are no larger-than-life screens, no computer-generated graphics, no state-of-the-art digital sound system. No drums, no fancy keyboard rig, no electric guitars, and no worship team with the latest brand of in-ear monitors. The chapel itself is cavernous and what few chairs and benches there are have been pushed along the walls. Most, a little over a thousand by my guess, sit on the floor.

The music of Taizé is vastly different from the whole of contemporary Christian music, featuring short, simple choruses with accessible but infectious melodies. Though simple, the lyrics are far from simplistic, taken straight from Scripture. Some are chanted or sung as a round. At first I was taken aback by how often each song is repeated in a typical Taizé service. About the fourth time around, I was ready to move on. Yet we weren't even halfway through! Because of their brevity and simplicity, Taizé choruses can be learned quickly. The idea is to set the songbook aside as soon as you can, sing from your heart, and let the words wash over you. The sooner I realized this, the more meaningful it was to repeat the choruses, each time letting them burrow deeper into my heart and soul.

Taizé services are contemplative and reverent. Worshipers enter the chapel quietly; no talking is allowed. Everyone sits in silence, waiting prayerfully for the service to begin. A few minutes of silence is also observed at some point during the service, most often after a Scripture reading.

Liturgy and responsive readings play a significant role at a Taizé service. Prayers are based on Scripture, well thought out, and well crafted—a welcome relief from some of the rambling, cliché-laden prayers some of us have been subjected to in church over the years. "Prayer around the cross" is offered once a week where a cross is laid flat over supports and worshipers are invited to gather around it and pray.

Beauty is also given ample consideration at Taizé. Though far from ostentatious, a large arrangement of candles surrounds the altar. Icons and other artwork adorn the walls. Four-part harmony lends its unique beauty to the singing of each worship song.

Finally, the Taizé community is deliberately multicultural. While there, I met Christians from Europe, Africa, North America, and the Far East. To accommodate this vast array of diversity, Scripture is read and songs are sung in a variety of languages.

What I took away from my time at Taizé was a greater appreciation for silence, beauty, and reverence during worship. I'm now more at ease when any worship leader asks me to sing a verse or chorus over and over. Each repetition invites me deeper into the meaning of the lyrics. Most importantly, I got a taste of multiethnic worship on a scale I had never experienced, leaving me hungry for more.

Unity in Diversity

The Bible teaches that the beauty and power of the church is that it is one body with many diverse members. "For just as the body is one and has many members, and all the members of the body, though many, are ... one body—Jews or Greeks, slaves or free—and all were made to drink of one Spirit" (1 Corinthians 12:12–13). Our diversity should be a source of strength. The renowned Russian Orthodox priest Father Alexander Men wrote, "And if in the past the Church split apart, it split precisely because people failed to understand that diversity and unity are compatible conditions. We need to understand this now. Yes, there will be diversity, but it need not turn into antagonistic, divisive groupings, or schisms and sects."[62] Our differences need not divide us.

There is unity in diversity because that which we have in common, redemption through the blood of Christ, is greater than our differences. By his death on the cross, Jesus reconciled all people to God and to each other. "For in him all the fullness of God was pleased to dwell, and through him to reconcile to himself all things, whether on earth or in heaven, making peace by the blood of his cross" (Colossians 1:19–20). All believers, regardless of race, are inextricably bound together in Christ.

The Bible charges us to continue Christ's "ministry of reconciliation" (2 Corinthians 5:18) and to be "eager to maintain the unity of the Spirit in the bond of peace" (Ephesians 4:3). You and I are to do everything in our power to preserve and protect the unity of our home church. That's why 1 Peter 3:8 encourages church people to "have unity of mind, sympathy ... love, a tender heart, and a humble mind" toward each other. Commenting on this verse, New Testament scholar C. E. B. Cranfield adds:

> The more seriously we take the New Testament, the more urgent and painful becomes our sense of the sinfulness of the divisions, and the more earnest our prayers and strivings after the peace and unity of the Church on earth. That does not mean that the like-mindedness we are to strive for is to be a drab uniformity of the sort beloved of bureaucrats. Rather is it to be a unity in which powerful tensions are held together by an over-mastering loyalty, and strong antipathies of race and colour, temperament and taste, social position and economic interest, are overcome in common worship and common obedience.[63]

A few years ago, at a worship conference, I experienced one of the most memorable examples of unity in diversity. Right before I was to speak, a group of musicians took the stage to lead worship. They were strikingly diverse. A gray-haired Caucasian woman in her sixties sat down at the piano. Four singers made their way to the front of the stage. On the far left stood a very large African-American man. Next to him was a petite young Norwegian-looking blonde. Beside her stood a slim African-American young man followed by a middle-aged white woman. The crowd was instantly quiet, curious to see what kind of sound would come from such a widely assorted crew. From their very first note, this group had us in the palms of their hands. They brought the house down with soulful renditions of authentic black gospel songs and spirituals. Those five musicians — diverse in age, weight, gender, and heritage — wove their differences into a beautiful, worship-filled expression of Christian unity.

In the end, a church's greatest accomplishment may not be its impressive attendance figures, massive budget, or inspiring architecture. The ultimate test of success may not be how many small groups we had or the number of missions trips we took, but whether we learned to worship together even though we're not all alike. Philippians 1:27 reminds us to stand firm "in one spirit, with one mind striving side by side for the faith of the gospel."

The choice is ours—we can allow diversity to produce unity or strife. When we choose unity, we are able to worship on earth like we will in heaven, standing side by side with Christians from all walks of life and from every tribe, nation, and tongue praising our great, glorious, and transcendent God.

Ponder and Apply

1 How has your culture and background shaped your views on worship and your taste in worship music?

2 What's your impression of the vision for multiethnic worship presented in this chapter?

3 Since diversity is not just a racial issue, in what other areas could Christians be more accepting and loving toward each other?

4 Do you have any broken relationships at church? Is there anyone with whom you need to reconcile? Anyone you need to forgive? If so, set up an appointment this week to meet and talk.

5 Do you have any additional thoughts or comments regarding the author's defense of Christian rap music and other innovations in worship? If so, explain.

FOR PASTORS AND WORSHIP LEADERS

There is much written these days for leaders about the multiethnic church, but I'd like to continue to focus on the subject as it pertains to worship and pose a few questions for consideration. In regard to racial diversity, does the mix of people you have on the platform every week (i.e., worship team, choir, those who give announcements, etc.) reflect the ethnic makeup of your congregation? Minorities do not feel welcome unless they see people like themselves in upfront leadership roles. Pastor Mark DeYmaz reminds church leaders to be more than just mindful of minorities, but to be proactively inclusive:

> Well-meaning believers will often describe themselves as open to diversity and to having anyone who so desires become a part of "their" church. However, the unintended obstacle to this otherwise sincere belief is a lack of proactive consideration of diverse individuals who may walk through the doors. The statement, "We would welcome anyone here," is in most cases more accurately translated, "We would welcome anyone here as long as they like who we are, what we do, and how we do it." In other words, "We welcome anyone to join us as long as they are willing to conform to our ways but don't expect us to conform to theirs!" And nowhere is this attitude more pronounced than in a congregation's approach to worship.
>
> To build a healthy multi-ethnic church, then, it is in worship that leaders must begin to promote a spirit of inclusion. For example, if the worship format in style and leadership is the same from week to week, it will appeal only to a certain segment of the population; thus a barrier (though perhaps unintended) is erected. Yet by diversifying its worship format —the songs that are sung, the way that they are done, and by whom—a church will demonstrate its (God's) heart for all people.[64]

Because diversity is more than just a racial issue, there are broader questions to consider as well: Do you accept only beautiful athletic-looking people on your worship team? Or do you have a variety of shapes and sizes, people from all walks of life, on the platform? Are there elements of your service that appeal to a wide variety of people?

I'm not advocating that you make diversity the sole agenda of your church. Instead, be a Bible-believing, Bible-teaching, Bible-following church and you'll automatically be inclined to include minorities because it's commanded throughout Scripture. Beyond that, achieving diversity in worship takes intentionality, courage, and vision. May the Lord grant you perseverance and strength of will as you exhort your congregation to set aside irrelevant differences and worship in the unity we have in Jesus Christ.

Let's Worship Like We're Already There

After John heard the great multitude in heaven singing God's praises loudly and enthusiastically, I bet his own practice of worship was never the same again. After seeing the Lord seated on his heavenly throne, high and exalted, I can't imagine Isaiah returning to his local synagogue and worshiping as he did before. So it is with us. After considering worship in heaven, how can any of us go back to business as usual in the way we worship? Theologian Allen P. Ross agrees:

> To lift up our hearts to that transcendent glory for even a moment will have a definite impact on the way we worship. If we even begin to comprehend the risen Christ in all his glory, or faintly hear the heavenly choirs that surround the throne with their anthems of praise or imagine what life in the presence of the Lord will be like, then we can never again be satisfied with worship as usual. We will always be striving to make our worship fit for glory.[65]

As you strive to make your worship "fit for glory," may you continue to sense the Holy Spirit leading you to:

- Make worship a priority.
- Establish a regular routine for private worship.

- Smash your idols.
- Worship amidst adversity.

When you go to church, may you continue to hear the Spirit's invitation to:

- Focus on God's attributes during corporate worship.
- Bring God your best worship.
- Set aside personal preferences.
- Embrace diversity.

Thanks to the vivid firsthand accounts from John and Isaiah, we can close our eyes whenever we want and picture worship in heaven: the magnificent colors, the glorious voices, the bright light. Those stunningly intriguing four living creatures and the elders clothed in pure white falling down before the Lamb. Myriads of angels and that great multitude, stretched out as far as the eye can see, from every nation, tribe, and tongue—all with faces to the ground. The sheer beauty of it all takes my breath away.

Sometimes as I'm poring over a psalm and my heart is stirred by a certain attribute of God, I remember that at that very moment, worship in heaven is in full swing. It happens at church too. While singing along with God's people, I'll realize that the most glorious worship of all is resounding throughout heaven at the same time. In those moments, I sense the Lord inviting me to do more than just gaze heavenward. God is inviting me to join in heaven's worship, to add my voice to the celestial choir. In fact, Ephesians 2:6 states that, because of Christ, we are already "seated ... in the heavenly places."

So let's worship as if we're already there. Let's worship God with a mighty voice as if we're already with him in paradise.

Names of God

Advocate (1 John 2:1)

Alpha and Omega,
the Beginning and the End
(Revelation 22:13)

Bread of Life (John 6:48)

Consuming Fire (Hebrews 12:29)

Creator (Genesis 1:1)

Deliverer (Romans 11:26)

Eternal King (Psalm 10:16)

Father (Deuteronomy 32:6)

Father of the Fatherless
(Psalm 68:5)

Friend (John 15:15)

Friend of Sinners
(Matthew 11:19)

Everlasting Father (Isaiah 9:6)

Everlasting God (Isaiah 40:28)

Giver of Every Good Gift
(James 1:17)

Giver of Life (John 5:21)

God Almighty (Genesis 17:1)

God of All Comfort
(2 Corinthians 1:3)

God of Endurance (Romans 15:5)

God of Encouragement
(Romans 15:5)

God of Glory (Psalm 29:3)

God of My Life (Psalm 42:8)

God of My Salvation
(Psalm 88:1)

God Who Sees (Genesis 16:13)

Good Shepherd (John 10:11)

Great and Awesome God
(Nehemiah 1:5)

Guide (Psalm 48:14)

Head of the Church
(Colossians 1:18)

Healer (Exodus 15:26)

Help in Times of Trouble
(Psalm 46:1)

Holy God (Isaiah 5:16)

Immanuel, God with Us
(Matthew 1:23)

Jealous (Exodus 34:14)

Judge (Judges 11:27)

King (Psalm 98:6)

King of Glory (Psalm 24:8)

King of Kings (1 Timothy 6:15)

Living God (Joshua 3:10)

Lord God (Genesis 2:4)

Lord of All (Romans 10:12)

Lord of Lords
(Deuteronomy 10:17)

Love (1 John 4:8)

Master (Luke 5:5)

Messiah (John 1:41)

Mighty God (Isaiah 10:21)

Most High God (Psalm 57:2)

My Deliverer (Psalm 18:2)

My Help (Psalm 63:7)

My Hope (Psalm 71:5)

My King (Psalm 68:24)

My Light (Psalm 27:1)

My Rock (Psalm 31:3)

My Salvation (Psalm 18:46)

My Shepherd (Psalm 23:1)

My Shield (Psalm 28:7)

My Strength (Psalm 59:9)

Name Above All Names
(Philippians 2:9)

Our Father (Isaiah 63:16)

Our Peace (Ephesians 2:14)

Our Righteousness
(Jeremiah 23:6)

Prince of Peace (Isaiah 9:6)

Protector (Psalm 68:5)

Provider (Genesis 22:14)

Redeemer (Isaiah 49:26)

Refuge (Psalm 62:8)

Rock (Deuteronomy 32:4)

Savior (Luke 1:47)

Shelter (Isaiah 25:4)

Sovereign Lord (Acts 4:24)

Stronghold (Psalm 9:9)

Sure Foundation (Isaiah 28:16)

Teacher (Matthew 26:18)

Truth (John 14:6)

The Way (John 14:6)

Upholder of My Life (Psalm 54:4)

Wonderful Counselor
(Isaiah 9:6)

Attributes of God

God is ...

   able (Ephesians 3:20)

   abounding in steadfast love and faithfulness (Exodus 34:6)

   all-knowing (Psalm 139:1–6)

   all-powerful (Jeremiah 32:17)

   attentive (Psalm 66:19)

   awesome (Deuteronomy 7:21)

   compassionate (James 5:11)

   eternal (Deuteronomy 33:27)

   ever-present (Acts 17:27)

   exalted (Psalm 18:46)

   faithful (2 Timothy 2:13)

   familiar with suffering (Isaiah 53:3)

   forgiving (Psalm 86:5)

   gentle (Matthew 11:29)

   glorious (Psalm 76:4)

   good (Titus 3:4)

   gracious (Psalm 111:4)

   great (Psalm 147:5)

   holy (Isaiah 6:3)

immense (Isaiah 40:12)

immutable (Hebrews 13:8)

incomparable (Psalm 89:6)

infinite (Psalm 90:1–2)

jealous (Exodus 20:5)

just (Psalm 75:1–7)

kind (Romans 2:4)

loving (Romans 8:38–39)

majestic (Psalm 8:1)

merciful (Exodus 34:6)

near (Acts 17:27)

patient (2 Peter 3:9)

perfect (Hebrews 7:28)

personal (2 Corinthians 6:16–18)

powerful (Ephesians 1:19)

relational (Revelation 3:20)

sovereign (1 Timothy 6:15)

steadfast (Psalm 25:6)

strong (Psalm 24:8)

transcendent (Psalm 113:4–5)

trustworthy (Psalm 25:2)

wise (Proverbs 3:19–20)

worthy (Revelation 4:11)

Notes

1. George Barna, *Revolution: Finding Vibrant Faith beyond the Walls of the Sanctuary* (Wheaton, Ill.: Tyndale, 2005), 31–32.

2. D. A. Carson, *Worship by the Book* (Grand Rapids: Zondervan, 2002), 31.

3. A. W. Tozer, *The Purpose of Man*, compiled and edited by James L. Snyder (Ventura, Calif.: Regal, 2009), 47.

4. A. W. Tozer, *Whatever Happened to Worship? A Call to True Worship* (Camp Hill, Penn.: Wing Spread, 2006), 94.

5. C. S. Lewis, *Reflections on the Psalms* (New York: Harcourt Brace, 1958), 95.

6. Ibid., 97.

7. N. T. Wright, *For All God's Worth: True Worship and the Calling of the Church* (Grand Rapids: Eerdmans, 1997), 7.

8. Mark Driscoll and Gerry Breshears, *Doctrine: What Christians Should Believe* (Wheaton, Ill., Crossway, 2010), 339.

9. *The ESV Study Bible, English Standard Version*, footnote on Ephesians 1:6 (Wheaton, Ill.: Crossway Bibles, 2008), 2262.

10. Noel Due, *Created for Worship: From Genesis to Revelation to You* (Fearn, Ross-shire, Scotland: Christian Focus, 2005), 19.

11. C. S. Lewis, *Letters to Malcolm: Chiefly on Prayer* (New York: Harcourt Brace, 1992), 75.

12. A. W. Tozer, *Whatever Happened to Worship?*, 56, 93.

13. William Law, *A Serious Call to a Devout and Holy Life* (Peabody, Mass.: Hendrickson, 2009), 162.

14. My "Daily Praise Offerings" are posted regularly at *www.heartoftheartist.org*.

15. A. W. Tozer, *The Purpose of Man: Designed to Worship* (Ventura, Calif.: Regal, 2009), 101.

16. R. C. Sproul, *A Taste of Heaven: Worship in the Light of Eternity* (Lake Mary, Fla.: Reformation Trust, 2006), 10.

17. A. W. Tozer, *Whatever Happened to Worship*, 41–42.

18. John Piper, *God's Passion for His Glory: Living the Vision of Jonathan Edwards* (Wheaton, Ill.: Crossway, 1998), 36.

19. A. W Tozer, *The Purpose of Man*, 55.

20. Timothy Keller, *Counterfeit Gods: The Empty Promises of Money, Sex, and Power, and the Only Hope That Matters* (New York: Dutton, 2009), xvii-xviii.

21. Francis Chan, with Danae Yankoski, *Crazy Love: Overwhelmed by a Relentless God* (Colorado Springs: David C. Cook, 2008), 96–97.

22. Timothy Keller, *Counterfeit Gods*, 165–166.

23. Francis Chan, with Danae Yankoski, *Crazy Love*, 96.

24. David Peterson, *Engaging with God: A Biblical Theology of Worship* (Downers Grove, Ill.: IVP Academic, 1992), 144.

25. Timothy Keller, *Counterfeit Gods*, 19–20.

26. Lewis E. Jones, *There Is Power in the Blood* (1899).

27. John Piper, *God's Passion for His Glory*, 47.

28. Carlo Carretto, *The God Who Comes* (London: Darton, Longman and Todd, 1974), 93.

29. Mark Batterson, *In a Pit with a Lion on a Snowy Day: How to Survive and Thrive When Opportunity Roars* (Colorado Springs, Multnomah, 2006), 67.

30. John MacArthur, *The Ultimate Priority* (Chicago: Moody Press, 1983), 2.

31. A. W. Tozer, *Whatever Happened to Worship?*, 13.

32. Randy Alcorn, *Heaven* (Carol Stream, Ill.: Tyndale, 2004), 224.

33. Matt Redman, *Facedown* (Ventura, Calif.: Regal, 2004), 23–24.

34. "Holy, Holy, Holy," Words: Reginald Heber (1826); Music: John B. Dykes (1861).

35. Jean M. Twenge and W. Keith Campbell, *The Narcissism Epidemic: Living in the Age of Entitlement* (New York: Free Press, division of Simon & Schuster, 2009), 30–31.

36. Ibid., 1.

37. D. A. Carson, *Worship by the Book* (Grand Rapids: Zondervan, 2002), 39.

38. Mark Batterson, *In a Pit with a Lion on a Snowy Day*, 69–70.

Notes

39. R. C. Sproul, *A Taste of Heaven*, 126.

40. Thomas Merton, *Thoughts in Solitude* (New York: Farrar, Straus and Giroux, 1958), 33.

41. C. S. Lewis, *Letters to Malcolm: Chiefly on Prayer* (New York: Harcourt Brace, 1992), 4.

42. John Piper, *God's Passion for His Glory*, 37.

43. James Strong, *Strong's Exhaustive Concordance* (Grand Rapids, Mich.: Baker, reprinted 1981), 114.

44. Ibid., 61.

45. John Piper, *God's Passion for His Glory*, 41.

46. Mark D. Roberts, *No Holds Barred: Wrestling with God in Prayer* (Colorado Springs: WaterBrook, 2005), 66.

47. William Law, *A Serious Call to a Devout and Holy Life* (Peabody, Mass.: Hendrickson, 2009), 175–176.

48. A. W. Tozer, *Whatever Happened to Worship?*, 82–83.

49. "Church Attendance," Barna Group: *www.barna.org*, 2006.

50. As reported in *Worship Leader*, "A Snapshot of Youth Today," September 2008, 29.

51. Sonja Steptoe/Bellflower, "In Touch with Jesus," *Time*, October 31, 2006.

52. "LifeWay Research Uncovers Reasons 18- to 22-Year-Olds Drop Out of Church" (April–May 2007), *LifeWay*: *www.lifeway.com/article/165949*.

53. Allen P. Ross, *Recalling the Hope of Glory: Biblical Worship from the Garden to the New Creation* (Grand Rapids: Kregel, 2006), 440.

54. Philip Schaff, *History of the Christian Church*, vol. 4 (Peabody, Mass.: Hendrickson, 2006), 439.

55. Based on "War (What Is It Good For)," by Norman Whitfield and Barrett Strong, 1969. Recorded by Edwin Starr in 1970 for Motown Records as well as Bruce Springsteen and the E Street Band in 1986.

56. N. C. Aizenman, "U.S. to Grow Grayer, More Diverse: Minorities Will Be Majority by 2042, Census Bureau Says," *Washington Post*: *www.washington post.com* (August 14, 2008).

57. To view Johnnie singing this song and read Pastor James's comments, go to *jamesmacdonald.com/blog/?p=2612*.

58. Brenda Aghaowa, *Praising in Black and White: Unity and Diversity in Christian Worship* (Cleveland: United Church Press, 1996), 41.

59. David A. Anderson, *Multicultural Ministry: Finding Your Church's Unique Rhythm*, (Grand Rapids: Zondervan, 2004), 106–107.

60. Justo L. Gonzalez, *¡Alabadle! Hispanic Christian Worship* (Nashville: Abingdon, 1996), 20–21.

61. Juana Bordas, *Salsa, Soul, and Spirit: Leadership for a Multicultural Age* (San Francisco: Berrett-Koehler, 2007), 45–46.

62. Alexander Men, *About Christ and the Church*, trans. Alexis Vinogradov (Torrance, Calif.: Oakwood, 1996), 40.

63. Quoted in William Barclay, *The New Daily Study Bible: The Letters of James and Peter* (Louisville, Ky.: Westminster John Knox Press, 2003), 260–61.

64. Mark DeYmaz, *Building a Healthy Multi-Ethnic Church: Mandate, Commitments, and Practices of a Diverse Congregation* (San Francisco: John Wiley & Sons, 2007), 109–10.

65. Allen P. Ross, *Recalling the Hope of Glory*, 473–74.

The Heart of the Artist

A Character-Building Guide for You and Your Ministry Team

Rory Noland

- Great for individuals and teams
- Includes provocative discussion
  questions

Over 100,000 sold

"I wish I had your gift!"

How do you handle those words as a creative artist? Somewhere between pride and self-abasement lies true humility — just one aspect of the balanced character God wants to instill in you as an actor, a musician, a visual artist, or other creative person involved in ministry. God is interested in your art and your heart.

The Heart of the Artist deals head-on with issues every person in an arts ministry faces:

- Servanthood versus stardom
- Excellence versus perfectionism
- The spiritual disciplines of the artist
- The artist in community ... and more

The Heart of the Artist will give you a better understanding of yourself and your unique place in the body of Christ. You'll find wisdom and encouragement that can help you survive the challenges and reap the rich joys of a ministry in the creative arts.

Available in stores and online!

ZONDERVAN®
.com

Thriving as an Artist in the Church

Hope and Help for You and Your Ministry Team

Rory Noland, Author of
The Heart of the Artist

- Great for individual or group use
- Includes provocative discussion questions and practical action steps
- Features four-color art plates and literary quotes

Thriving as an Artist in the Church is a practical guide, full of wisdom and pastoral guidance, that will help you surmount the obstacles and flourish in your ministry. It's packed with examples, discussion questions, personal action steps, and mega-doses of encouragement. Most important, it tackles the real-life issues every artist in the church has to deal with:

- Sustaining passion
- Developing key relational skills
- Dealing with rejection and failure
- Cultivating confidence
- Resolving artistic differences
- And much more!

Written by an artist for artists, this book will help make your ministry experience sustainable and life-giving so you can fall in love with the church all over again.

Available in stores and online!

The Worshiping Artist

Equipping You and
Your Ministry Team to
Lead Others in Worship

Rory Noland, Author of
The Heart of the Artist

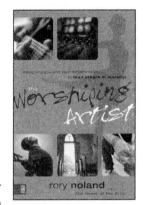

Whether you serve as a vocalist, instrumentalist, technician, dancer, actor, or in some other role, you know what a blessing it is to serve on your church's worship team. But you also know that some days you're more technically prepared than you are spiritually prepared for the ministry of leading others in worship. In the midst of rehearsals, setup, and myriad distractions, not to mention the busyness of daily life, it's easy to miss the forest for the trees. How can you and your fellow team members be prepared to worship in spirit and truth as well as lead others in worship with integrity?

With thirty years of experience in leading worship, Rory Noland knows the issues — in both the private life of the worship team member and the public ministry of a worship team. In this readable book, he offers practical insights on how to

- Grow as a private worshiper
- Encounter the character of God during worship
- Respond to the character of God during worship
- Be transformed by the character of God
- Learn from ancient worship leaders ... and more.

The Worshiping Artist is ideal to read either by yourself or as a team.

Share Your Thoughts

With the Author: Your comments will be forwarded to the author when you send them to *zauthor@zondervan.com*.

With Zondervan: Submit your review of this book by writing to *zreview@zondervan.com*.

Free Online Resources at

www.zondervan.com

Zondervan AuthorTracker: Be notified whenever your favorite authors publish new books, go on tour, or post an update about what's happening in their lives at www.zondervan.com/authortracker.

Daily Bible Verses and Devotions: Enrich your life with daily Bible verses or devotions that help you start every morning focused on God. Visit www.zondervan.com/newsletters.

Free Email Publications: Sign up for newsletters on Christian living, academic resources, church ministry, fiction, children's resources, and more. Visit www.zondervan.com/newsletters.

Zondervan Bible Search: Find and compare Bible passages in a variety of translations at www.zondervanbiblesearch.com.

Other Benefits: Register to receive online benefits like coupons and special offers, or to participate in research.

ZONDERVAN.com/
AUTHOR**TRACKER**
follow your favorite authors